The Homelessness Challenge: Could You, Would You, Make a Difference?"

TABLE OF CONTENTS

INTRODUCTION

Introduction: The Homelessness Challenge

Homelessness is an issue that often remains hidden in the shadows of our society. It is a pervasive crisis that affects millions of individuals worldwide, and yet, it's a topic that is seldom discussed openly. In this book, we will embark on a journey into the heart of homelessness, aiming to shed light on the unseen realities, challenges, and potential solutions to this pressing issue.

As you hold this book in your hands, you might wonder why we've chosen such a provocative title: "The Homelessness Challenge: Could You, Would You, Make a Difference?" The answer is both simple and profound. We want you, the reader, to not only understand the complexities of homelessness but also to experience it—albeit in a controlled and temporary manner. We want you to step into the shoes of those who grapple with homelessness every day, if only for a brief moment, in the hope that it will ignite empathy, spark action, and lead to positive change.

This book is divided into two distinct acts, each with its own focus and purpose. In Act 1, "Understanding Homelessness," we will delve deep into the multifaceted world of homelessness. We'll explore the many faces of homelessness, dissect the root causes, and examine its profound impact on individuals and communities. We'll also introduce you to the brave individuals who have experienced homelessness and share their stories, dispelling myths and challenging stereotypes.

In Act 2, "Making a Difference," we'll transition from understanding to action. Here, we'll present a unique challenge: the "30-Day Homelessness Challenge." You'll have the opportunity to immerse yourself in the daily struggles faced by homeless individuals, albeit in a controlled and temporary manner. This experience is designed to cultivate empathy, encourage reflection, and inspire you to make a difference in the lives of those who are experiencing homelessness.

But before we embark on this journey together, it's crucial to understand our motivations and intentions. Our goal is not to romanticize homelessness or trivialize its challenges. Homelessness is a complex issue with no easy answers, and our approach is one of deep respect for the individuals who endure it. We aim to foster understanding, compassion, and meaningful change.

Let's begin our exploration by peeling back the layers of this issue and understanding what homelessness truly entails. In the following chapters of Act 1, we'll reveal the "Unseen Realities" and "Homelessness Unveiled." We'll delve into the causes, consequences, and the deep-seated stigma that often surrounds homelessness. By the end of Act 1, you will have a solid foundation upon which to build your understanding.

Act 2 is where we challenge you to step outside of your comfort zone and experience a slice of homelessness. We'll provide you with guidelines, reflections, and a structured approach to a 30-day experience. Throughout this journey, you will gain insights that transcend statistics and headlines, gaining a visceral understanding of the daily hardships faced by those without stable housing.

We'll also examine the root causes of homelessness, the interconnected issues of mental health and addiction, and the systemic barriers that perpetuate this crisis. Through these chapters, we hope to inspire you to become an advocate for change.

By the time we reach the conclusion of this book, we aim to leave you not only with a deepened understanding of homelessness but also with a sense of purpose. We want you to answer the question posed in our title: "Could You, Would You, Make a Difference?" We believe that the answer is a resounding "Yes," and we will equip you with the knowledge, empathy, and resources to do just that.

The journey ahead is both enlightening and challenging. It will require an open heart, a willingness to confront uncomfortable truths, and a commitment to making a positive impact in your community and beyond. So, as we embark on this exploration of homelessness and empathy, let us remember that our collective efforts have the power to transform lives and create a more compassionate society.

Welcome to "The Homelessness Challenge." Let's begin.

Act 1: Understanding Homelessness

Welcome to Act 1 of our journey, "Understanding Homelessness." In this act, we will illuminate the intricate layers of an issue that often remains concealed in the shadows of our society. Our goal is to equip you with a comprehensive understanding of homelessness, its diverse faces, the underlying causes, and its profound impact on individuals and communities.

The first step in addressing any complex problem is to unravel its mysteries, to shine a light on the unseen realities that lie beneath the surface. Homelessness is no exception. It's a multifaceted issue, one that defies simple categorization or easy solutions. To truly comprehend it, we must embark on a journey of exploration and empathy.

In the opening chapter, "Unseen Realities," we will venture into the heart of homelessness. We'll explore its presence in our communities, often invisible to the casual observer, and reveal the stark contrast between the perceptions and the realities of those experiencing homelessness. By the end of this chapter, you'll begin to grasp the scale of the challenge we face.

Chapter 2, "Homelessness Unveiled," takes us further into the lives of those who grapple with homelessness daily. We'll hear their voices, share their stories, and gain an unfiltered glimpse into their world. It's an opportunity to break through the barriers of preconceived notions and stereotypes, to recognize the shared humanity that connects us all.

To address a problem effectively, we must first understand its origins and causes. Chapter 3, "Beyond the Streets," delves into the root causes of homelessness. We'll examine the systemic factors, personal challenges, and societal dynamics that contribute to this crisis. By doing so, we lay the groundwork for meaningful change.

Chapter 4, "From Shelter to Hope," transitions from understanding to empathy. Here, we'll prepare you for the experiential journey that awaits in Act 2. We'll offer insights into the personal preparations required for the Homelessness Challenge and emphasize the importance of approaching this endeavor with an open heart and a commitment to learning.

Finally, in Chapter 5, "Faces of Resilience," we will introduce you to the inspiring individuals who have not only survived homelessness but thrived in its face. Their stories are testaments to the resilience of the human spirit and the capacity for transformation. These narratives will serve as beacons of hope and exemplars of what is possible when individuals and communities come together.

As we embark on this journey of understanding, let us remember that knowledge is the first step toward meaningful change. By the end of Act 1, you will possess the insights and awareness necessary to confront the challenges of homelessness head-on. You will be better equipped to respond with empathy, compassion, and the determination to make a difference.

So, let us begin this expedition into the heart of homelessness, ready to uncover the unseen realities, challenge our assumptions, and emerge with a deeper understanding of the issue that binds us all together.

Welcome to Act 1: "Understanding Homelessness."

Chapter 1: Unseen Realities

Section 1: Introduction to Homelessness

Homelessness, like an iceberg, reveals only a fraction of its true magnitude. It is a crisis that often remains hidden in the shadows of our society, concealed from our daily lives. In this chapter, we embark on a journey to unveil the unseen realities of homelessness, starting with a basic understanding of what it truly means to be homeless.

Homelessness Defined

At its core, homelessness signifies living without a stable and adequate place to call home. It is not a mere lack of shelter; it's a state of insecurity, vulnerability, and uncertainty. Homelessness doesn't discriminate based on age, gender, or socioeconomic status. It can affect anyone, often as a result of a combination of factors, some within an individual's control, while others are beyond it.

To put it simply, homelessness means not having a place to go when night falls. It's the absence of that safe, warm space where one can find refuge from the world's storms, both literal and metaphorical. Homelessness means not having a bed to sleep in, a kitchen to cook a meal, or a bathroom to use with privacy. But it's not just about physical comfort; it's about security, stability, and the ability to plan for tomorrow.

The reality of homelessness extends beyond the lack of a roof over one's head. It encompasses the challenges of finding food, maintaining hygiene, accessing healthcare, and securing one's belongings. It's about navigating the complexities of life without the stability that a home provides.

Diverse Faces of Homelessness

Homelessness doesn't adhere to a single stereotype. It encompasses a wide spectrum of experiences, from families with children struggling to make ends meet, to single adults facing addiction or mental health challenges. Veterans, youth, and LGBTQ+ individuals also find themselves grappling with homelessness. Even older adults and survivors of natural disasters can fall into homelessness. It's essential to recognize that the face of homelessness is diverse, and each person's story is unique.

1. **Families in Crisis**: Families experiencing homelessness are one of the most heart-wrenching facets of this issue. It's a painful paradox—the very institution that should provide safety and stability, the family, becomes the gateway to homelessness for many. Economic hardship, job loss, or the lack of affordable housing often push families to the brink of homelessness. Parents face the excruciating choice of prioritizing housing or providing other essential needs for their children.
2. **Single Adults**: Single individuals, both men and women, make up a significant portion of the homeless population. Their paths to homelessness vary—some struggle with addiction, others with mental health challenges, while some simply face economic difficulties. Regardless of the reasons, they share the experience of navigating life without the security of a permanent home.
3. **Veterans**: The sight of homeless veterans is a stark reminder of the challenges faced by those who have served their country. Veterans experiencing homelessness may grapple with post-traumatic stress disorder (PTSD), substance abuse, or other issues related to their service. Addressing veteran homelessness is a moral imperative and a reflection of our societal commitment to those who have sacrificed for our nation.

4. **Youth and LGBTQ+ Individuals**: Homelessness among young people is a particularly heartbreaking issue. LGBTQ+ youth, in particular, face a higher risk of homelessness due to family rejection and discrimination. These young individuals often become "hidden homeless," couch-surfing, or staying with friends to avoid the dangers of street life.
5. **Elderly Homelessness**: As individuals age, they become more vulnerable to homelessness. Fixed incomes, health issues, and the lack of affordable housing can force older adults into homelessness. The challenges faced by elderly homeless individuals are compounded by their age, making it even more difficult to escape the cycle of homelessness.
6. **Survivors of Natural Disasters**: Homelessness is not always a result of economic hardship or personal struggles. Natural disasters, such as hurricanes, earthquakes, wildfires, or floods, can displace entire communities, leaving individuals and families without homes. These survivors face the additional trauma of rebuilding their lives from the ground up.

Each of these faces represents a unique aspect of homelessness, and yet, they are all interconnected by the shared experience of housing instability. To truly understand the issue, we must recognize the diversity of experiences and backgrounds within the homeless population. As we explore these different faces of homelessness, we can begin to appreciate the individual stories that form the broader narrative of this crisis.

Root Causes

Understanding homelessness requires us to look beyond the immediate circumstances and examine the root causes that drive individuals and families into homelessness. It's a complex web of interrelated factors, often involving a combination of personal, systemic, and economic challenges.

1. **Economic Instability**: One of the primary drivers of homelessness is economic instability. Job loss, underemployment, or low wages can push individuals and families to the brink of homelessness. The inability to cover rent or basic living expenses can result in eviction and the loss of housing.

Economic instability is not a distant issue affecting only a small portion of the population. It's a vulnerability that many of us are just one unexpected event away from experiencing. A sudden medical crisis, an unexpected layoff, or a family emergency can quickly disrupt the delicate balance of income and expenses, leading to housing instability.

The cost of housing has outpaced wage growth in many regions, creating a chasm between what individuals earn and what it takes to secure safe and stable housing. The term "affordable housing" has become an elusive dream for millions, forcing them to make painful choices between paying for housing and covering other essential needs, such as food, transportation, and healthcare.

2. **Lack of Affordable Housing**: In many regions, the cost of housing far exceeds the income levels of low and moderate-income individuals and families. The shortage of affordable housing options forces people to make impossible choices between paying for shelter or other essential needs like food and healthcare.

Affordable housing isn't a mere policy issue; it's a fundamental human right. The absence of affordable housing options results in a cycle of housing instability that is difficult to break. When individuals are unable to find housing they can afford, they may be forced into overcrowded living conditions, unsafe neighborhoods, or homelessness.

3. **Mental Health Challenges**: Mental health issues are prevalent among the homeless population. Conditions such as schizophrenia, bipolar disorder, depression, and post-traumatic stress disorder (PTSD) can contribute to homelessness when individuals lack access to mental health services or stable housing environments.

Mental health challenges are complex, often intertwined with other factors like substance abuse, trauma, or economic hardship. Many individuals experiencing homelessness face a lack of access to adequate mental health care, leaving them vulnerable to the cyclical nature of homelessness.

4. **Substance Abuse**: Substance abuse is both a cause and a consequence of homelessness. Individuals struggling with addiction may find it difficult to maintain employment and stable housing, while the harsh realities of homelessness can lead to increased substance use as a means of coping.

Substance abuse can exacerbate homelessness by eroding one's support network, straining relationships, and affecting physical and mental health. It's a vicious cycle where homelessness and addiction feed into each other, making it even more challenging for individuals to break free from the grip of homelessness.

5. **Domestic Violence**: Victims of domestic violence often flee their homes to escape abusive situations, resulting in homelessness. The absence of safe, affordable housing options for survivors can further exacerbate their vulnerability.

Survivors of domestic violence face the excruciating choice of staying in an abusive environment or becoming homeless. This cruel dilemma underscores the importance of not only addressing homelessness but also providing a safe haven for those escaping violence.

6. **Systemic Factors**: Broader systemic issues, such as systemic racism, discrimination, and disparities in access to education and employment opportunities, can disproportionately affect marginalized communities, increasing their risk of homelessness.

Systemic factors create barriers that hinder access to stable housing and economic opportunities. For example, communities of color often face discriminatory practices in housing, education, and employment, leading to higher rates of poverty and homelessness within these communities.

Inadequate social safety nets and a lack of affordable healthcare can exacerbate the challenges faced by individuals experiencing homelessness. It's a vicious cycle where systemic inequities perpetuate homelessness, making it an issue that extends far beyond individual circumstances.

7. **Family Dynamics**: In some cases, strained family dynamics can lead to homelessness, particularly among youth. Family rejection, conflict, or a lack of support can force young individuals to leave their homes, leading to a life of instability.

The experience of homelessness can be particularly traumatic for youth, as they often lack the life skills and resources needed to navigate the challenges of life on the streets. Their vulnerability underscores the urgent need for support systems and resources tailored to the unique needs of youth experiencing homelessness.

Understanding these root causes is essential for developing effective strategies to address homelessness. It's not enough to provide temporary shelter or assistance; we must also work to dismantle the systemic issues that perpetuate housing instability.

Myths and Stereotypes

Homelessness is plagued by myths and stereotypes that oversimplify its complexities. Challenging these misconceptions is essential for gaining a deeper understanding of the crisis and responding to it with empathy and compassion.

1. **Myth: Homelessness is a Choice**: One common misconception is that homelessness is a result of personal choice or laziness. This myth ignores the intricate web of factors, including economic hardship, mental health challenges, and systemic inequities, that can lead to homelessness. No one chooses to be homeless.
2. **Myth: All Homeless Individuals Are Unemployed**: Another prevailing myth is that homeless individuals are all unemployed. In reality, many individuals experiencing homelessness do work, but their wages are often insufficient to cover the high cost of housing.
3. **Myth: Homelessness is Only a Big City Issue**: Homelessness is not confined to major urban centers. While it may be more visible in larger cities, homelessness exists in suburban and rural areas as well. The lack of affordable housing and support services is a nationwide problem.
4. **Myth: All Homeless Individuals Are Addicted to Drugs or Alcohol**: Substance abuse is indeed a challenge among homeless individuals, but it is not the sole cause of homelessness. Many people experiencing homelessness struggle with addiction as a way of coping with the harsh realities of life on the streets.
5. **Myth: Homelessness is a Temporary Problem**: For some individuals, homelessness may be a temporary setback. However, for many others, it becomes a long-term struggle. The longer someone experiences homelessness, the more difficult it becomes to escape its cycle.
6. **Myth: Homeless Individuals Don't Want Help**: This myth assumes that homeless individuals are resistant to assistance. In reality, many want to escape homelessness but face barriers such as a lack of affordable housing, limited access to mental health services, and discrimination.
7. **Myth: Homeless Individuals Are Dangerous**: Stereotypes often portray homeless individuals as dangerous or criminal. The majority are not, and many homeless individuals are victims of crimes themselves. It's essential to avoid stigmatizing this vulnerable population.

8. **Myth: Homelessness is an Intractable Problem**: While homelessness is a complex issue, it is not insurmountable. With effective policies, increased affordable housing, and robust support services, we can make significant progress in addressing homelessness.

Challenging these myths and stereotypes is a critical step in fostering empathy and understanding. By dispelling these misconceptions, we can pave the way for more compassionate and effective responses to homelessness.

As we progress through this chapter, our aim is to bring the unseen realities of homelessness into focus. By understanding its multifaceted nature and the factors that contribute to it, we can pave the way for empathy, awareness, and ultimately, positive change.

1.1: Homelessness Defined

At its core, homelessness is a complex and multifaceted issue that transcends mere statistics and headlines. To truly understand it, we must begin with a clear and compassionate definition.

The Essence of Homelessness: Homelessness is not just the absence of a physical roof over one's head; it's the void of a stable and adequate place to call home. It's an experience marked by insecurity, vulnerability, and uncertainty, which can rob individuals of their dignity and hope. It disrupts the basic human need for shelter, safety, and stability.

Imagine for a moment the fundamental aspects of your daily life: a bed to sleep in, a kitchen to prepare a meal, a bathroom for privacy and hygiene, and a secure space to keep your belongings. These are the basic elements of a stable home, and homelessness means not having these essentials.

The Spectrum of Homelessness: Homelessness is a spectrum, encompassing various living situations that lack stability. It's not limited to those we see sleeping on the streets, though that is a visible facet of the crisis. The spectrum includes individuals and families living in shelters, temporary accommodations, vehicles, or couch-surfing from one friend's house to another.

Consider the mother with two children who cannot afford the rent and moves her family between overcrowded apartments, never knowing when they might be asked to leave. Or the young adult who sleeps in their car because they cannot find affordable housing. They, too, are experiencing homelessness, though it may not fit the stereotypical image.

A Crisis Without Boundaries: Homelessness knows no boundaries—geographic, demographic, or social. It affects people from all walks of life. It disregards age, gender, and socioeconomic status. It can strike anyone, often due to a combination of factors, some within their control, while others are beyond it.

Homelessness isn't an exclusive club; it's a challenge that can befall individuals who, not long ago, lived in stable homes, held jobs, and had dreams for the future. The harsh reality is that many individuals experiencing homelessness were just one unexpected event away from losing their homes—a sudden medical bill, a job loss, or a family crisis.

The Emotional Toll: Beyond the physical challenges, homelessness takes an emotional toll. It inflicts feelings of shame, desperation, and despair. The uncertainty of where to sleep tonight, where to find food tomorrow, and how to access healthcare weighs heavily on the psyche.

Imagine the emotional turmoil of a child who, after being asked to leave their temporary shelter each morning, heads to school with no place to return to afterward. Or the single parent who, every night, tells their children that everything will be okay while struggling to hold back tears. These are the emotional realities of homelessness that often remain unseen.

A Crisis with No Simple Solutions: Homelessness is not a one-size-fits-all problem, and there are no quick fixes. It's a crisis that requires multifaceted solutions that address the root causes, provide immediate relief, and promote long-term stability. Homelessness necessitates compassion, empathy, and a comprehensive understanding of the diverse experiences it encompasses.

As we journey further into the heart of homelessness, we'll explore the different faces it wears, the root causes that underlie it, and the misconceptions that often shroud it. Our goal is not only to inform but to foster empathy and inspire action in addressing this pressing issue.

1.2: The Diverse Faces of Homelessness

To truly understand the depth of homelessness, we must recognize that it wears many faces. It is a crisis that affects a wide spectrum of individuals, each with a unique story of struggle, resilience, and hope. In this section, we shed light on some of the diverse faces of homelessness, dispelling the notion that it fits a single mold.

1. Families in Crisis

One of the most heart-wrenching aspects of homelessness is the impact it has on families. Families experiencing homelessness often find themselves caught in the relentless cycle of economic hardship, job loss, and the unaffordability of housing. For parents, it's a relentless struggle to provide for their children while navigating the uncertainty of where they will sleep each night.

Imagine a mother's despair as she searches for a safe place for her children to lay their heads, night after night. Or a father's frustration as he juggles the responsibility of finding a stable home with the daily demands of parenting. These families are not defined by their homelessness; they are defined by their strength and determination to create a better future for their children.

2. Single Adults

Single adults, both men and women, form a significant portion of the homeless population. Their paths to homelessness vary widely—some battle addiction, others confront mental health challenges, while some simply face economic difficulties that push them to the brink of homelessness. Regardless of the reasons, they share the experience of navigating life without the security of a permanent home.

Consider the individual who lost their job due to unforeseen circumstances, rapidly depleting their savings until they could no longer afford rent. Or the person who struggled with undiagnosed mental health issues, unable to access the care they needed to maintain stability. These single adults represent a diverse group of individuals who, despite their hardships, retain their dignity and resilience.

3. Veterans

The sight of homeless veterans is a poignant reminder of the challenges faced by those who have served their country. Veterans experiencing homelessness may grapple with post-traumatic stress disorder (PTSD), substance abuse, or other issues related to their service. Addressing veteran homelessness is a moral imperative and a reflection of our societal commitment to those who have sacrificed for our nation.

Imagine the irony of a veteran who served their country with honor but returns home to find themselves without a place to live. The struggles they face are not a reflection of their dedication but a stark reminder of the gaps in the support systems designed to aid them.

4. Youth and LGBTQ+ Individuals

Homelessness among young people is a particularly heartbreaking issue. LGBTQ+ youth, in particular, face a higher risk of homelessness due to family rejection and discrimination. These young individuals often become "hidden homeless," couch-surfing, or staying with friends to avoid the dangers of street life.

Picture the LGBTQ+ teenager who, after coming out to their family, is met with rejection and hostility, forcing them to leave their home in search of acceptance and safety. Or the young adult who, lacking a support system, becomes homeless while still in the formative years of their life.

5. Elderly Homelessness

As individuals age, they become more vulnerable to homelessness. Fixed incomes, health issues, and the lack of affordable housing can force older adults into homelessness. The challenges faced by elderly homeless individuals are compounded by their age, making it even more difficult to escape the cycle of homelessness.

Imagine the senior citizen who worked diligently throughout their life, only to find themselves without a stable home in their retirement years. They deserve a secure and dignified place to live, just like anyone else.

6. Survivors of Natural Disasters

Homelessness is not always a result of economic hardship or personal struggles. Natural disasters, such as hurricanes, earthquakes, wildfires, or floods, can displace entire communities, leaving individuals and families without homes. These survivors face the additional trauma of rebuilding their lives from the ground up.

Picture the devastation of a community after a catastrophic event, where homes are reduced to rubble, and families are left with nothing. These survivors did not choose homelessness; it was thrust upon them by forces beyond their control.

Each of these faces represents a unique aspect of homelessness, and yet, they are all interconnected by the shared experience of housing instability. To truly understand the issue, we must recognize the diversity of experiences and backgrounds within the homeless population. As we explore these different faces of homelessness, we can begin to appreciate the individual stories that form the broader narrative of this crisis.

Understanding the diverse faces of homelessness is a crucial step toward empathy and action. It dispels the misconception that homelessness is a monolithic problem with a one-size-fits-all solution. Instead, it underscores the need for a multifaceted approach that addresses the unique challenges faced by different segments of the homeless population.

1.3: Causes and Factors

To effectively address homelessness, we must delve deeper into its root causes. It's a complex web of interrelated factors, some within an individual's control, while others are systemic and societal challenges. Understanding these causes is essential for developing holistic strategies to combat homelessness.

1. Economic Instability

One of the primary drivers of homelessness is economic instability. Many individuals and families are just one paycheck away from homelessness. Job loss, underemployment, or low wages can push people to the brink of financial ruin, making it impossible to cover rent or basic living expenses.

Consider the story of a hardworking individual who loses their job due to unforeseen circumstances. With bills piling up and no safety net to rely on, they are forced to make the difficult choice between paying rent and putting food on the table. This scenario is not an isolated incident but a reality for millions of people.

2. Lack of Affordable Housing

In many regions, the cost of housing has skyrocketed, far outpacing wage growth. The shortage of affordable housing options has become a crisis in its own right. For low and moderate-income individuals and families, finding housing they can afford is a Herculean task.

Imagine a family struggling to secure stable housing in a market where rents are exorbitant and affordable units are scarce. The stress of juggling rent payments with other essential needs can lead to housing instability, even for those who work tirelessly to make ends meet.

3. Mental Health Challenges

Mental health issues are prevalent among the homeless population. Conditions such as schizophrenia, bipolar disorder, depression, and post-traumatic stress disorder (PTSD) can contribute to homelessness when individuals lack access to mental health services or stable housing environments.

Imagine an individual battling undiagnosed or untreated mental health issues, unable to access the care they need. The symptoms of their condition may lead to difficulties in maintaining employment and relationships, eventually resulting in housing instability.

4. Substance Abuse

Substance abuse is both a cause and a consequence of homelessness. Individuals struggling with addiction may find it difficult to maintain employment and stable housing, while the harsh realities of homelessness can lead to increased substance use as a means of coping.

Consider the spiral that many face: addiction leads to job loss, which leads to homelessness, which further fuels addiction as a way to numb the pain of living on the streets. Breaking free from this cycle requires not only addressing substance abuse but also providing stable housing and support.

5. Domestic Violence

Victims of domestic violence often flee their homes to escape abusive situations, resulting in homelessness. The absence of safe, affordable housing options for survivors can further exacerbate their vulnerability.

Imagine a person who must make the agonizing choice between staying in an abusive environment or becoming homeless. It's a choice that no one should have to make, underscoring the critical need for safe spaces and support systems for survivors.

6. Systemic Factors

Broader systemic issues, such as systemic racism, discrimination, and disparities in access to education and employment opportunities, can disproportionately affect marginalized communities, increasing their risk of homelessness.

Systemic factors create barriers that hinder access to stable housing and economic opportunities. For example, communities of color often face discriminatory practices in housing, education, and employment, leading to higher rates of poverty and homelessness within these communities.

7. Inadequate Social Safety Nets

Inadequate social safety nets and a lack of affordable healthcare can exacerbate the challenges faced by individuals experiencing homelessness. When individuals do not have access to essential services and support, it becomes exceedingly difficult for them to break free from the cycle of homelessness.

Imagine a healthcare system where individuals cannot access mental health services or treatment for chronic illnesses. When these individuals also lack stable housing, their health deteriorates further, perpetuating their homelessness.

Understanding these root causes is essential for developing effective strategies to address homelessness. It's not enough to provide temporary shelter or assistance; we must also work to dismantle the systemic issues that perpetuate housing instability.

By confronting these causes head-on, we can pave the way for comprehensive solutions that promote stable housing, mental health support, addiction treatment, and economic opportunity. In doing so, we can begin to untangle the complex web of factors that contribute to homelessness and work toward a society where everyone has a place to call home.

1.4: Myths and Stereotypes

Homelessness is plagued by myths and stereotypes that oversimplify its complexities and hinder our ability to address it effectively. Dispelling these misconceptions is vital for fostering empathy, understanding, and meaningful action.

1. Myth: Homelessness is a Choice

One common misconception about homelessness is that it is a result of personal choice or laziness. This myth suggests that individuals experiencing homelessness have intentionally chosen this path. In reality, homelessness is rarely a choice. It is typically the outcome of a combination of factors, including economic hardship, mental health challenges, and systemic issues.

Imagine the single parent who lost their job due to circumstances beyond their control, or the individual facing untreated mental health issues that affect their ability to maintain employment. These are not choices but rather challenges that have led to housing instability.

2. Myth: All Homeless Individuals Are Unemployed

Another prevalent myth is the assumption that homeless individuals are all unemployed. While employment status varies among homeless individuals, many do work. However, their wages are often insufficient to cover the high cost of housing. This myth highlights the discrepancy between wages and the cost of living in many regions.

Picture the individual who works multiple part-time jobs just to make ends meet but still cannot afford stable housing. They are not unemployed, yet they are trapped in the cycle of homelessness due to economic challenges.

3. Myth: Homelessness is Only a Big City Issue

While homelessness may be more visible in major urban centers, it is not confined to cities. Homelessness is a nationwide problem that affects suburban and rural areas as well. The lack of affordable housing and support services is a challenge that extends beyond metropolitan areas.

Imagine a small town where homelessness exists but often goes unnoticed. In these communities, individuals and families may struggle silently, lacking access to the resources available in larger cities.

4. Myth: All Homeless Individuals Are Addicted to Drugs or Alcohol

Substance abuse is indeed a challenge among homeless individuals, but it is not the sole cause of homelessness. Many people experiencing homelessness struggle with addiction as a way of coping with the harsh realities of life on the streets. Substance abuse can be both a cause and a consequence of homelessness, making it a complex issue to address.

Consider the person who turns to drugs or alcohol as a way to numb the pain of their circumstances, and how this coping mechanism can further exacerbate their homelessness. It's essential to approach substance abuse within the context of homelessness with compassion and understanding.

5. Myth: Homelessness is a Temporary Problem

While some individuals may experience temporary homelessness due to a short-term crisis, for many others, it becomes a long-term struggle. The longer someone experiences homelessness, the more difficult it becomes to escape its cycle. Over time, individuals may face additional challenges, such as deteriorating physical and mental health, making it even harder to secure stable housing.

Imagine the individual who initially lost their home due to a job loss but, after months or years of instability, faces new barriers to housing due to their extended homelessness.

6. Myth: Homeless Individuals Don't Want Help

This myth assumes that homeless individuals are resistant to assistance and prefer to remain homeless. In reality, many individuals want to escape homelessness but face significant barriers, such as a lack of affordable housing, limited access to mental health services, and discrimination.

Consider the individual who seeks help at a shelter or outreach program, only to find that available resources are insufficient to address their needs. Their desire for assistance is genuine, but systemic challenges hinder their path to stability.

7. Myth: Homeless Individuals Are Dangerous

Stereotypes often portray homeless individuals as dangerous or criminal. While some individuals may engage in illegal activities out of desperation, the majority are not dangerous. In fact, many homeless individuals are victims of crimes themselves, facing the dangers of life on the streets.

Imagine the vulnerability of a homeless person who must navigate the challenges of finding food, shelter, and safety while constantly aware of the risks they face. These individuals are not inherently dangerous but are often in need of protection and support.

8. Myth: Homelessness is an Intractable Problem

While homelessness is a complex issue, it is not insurmountable. With effective policies, increased affordable housing, and robust support services, we can make significant progress in addressing homelessness. This myth can discourage individuals and communities from taking action, but history has shown that positive change is possible when the right resources and commitment are in place.

By challenging these myths and stereotypes, we can begin to see homelessness as the complex and multifaceted issue it truly is. This understanding is the foundation for developing compassionate and effective responses to homelessness that prioritize empathy, dignity, and lasting solutions.

Section 2: The Struggles of Daily Life

"When you have exhausted all possibilities, remember this: you haven't." - Thomas Edison

Homelessness is not static; it's an ongoing battle to meet basic needs with limited resources. Here, we delve into the daily struggles on the streets, exploring the quest for food, the fragile sanctuary of sleep, the importance of hygiene, and the loneliness that often accompanies homelessness.

2.1: The Quest for Food

Hunger is a constant companion for many experiencing homelessness. This part takes an in-depth look at the daily quest for sustenance, from visits to soup kitchens to ingenious strategies employed to secure a meal.

Imagine shadowing an individual as they navigate the city, seeking out food pantries and community meal programs. Each meal becomes a lifeline, a brief respite from the gnawing hunger that accompanies life on the streets.

2.2: The Fragile Sanctuary of Sleep

Sleep is a precious commodity for the homeless, often elusive and disrupted by the harsh realities of street life. We explore the challenges of finding a safe place to rest, the dangers of exposure, and the toll sleep deprivation takes on physical and mental health.

Picture an individual with only a thin tent for shelter, ever vigilant against theft or assault. The nights are fraught with uncertainty, where safety is an elusive dream.

2.3: The Importance of Hygiene

Maintaining personal hygiene is a fundamental aspect of dignity, yet it is a luxury that many homeless individuals struggle to attain. In this section, we delve into the daily efforts to stay clean and the lack of access to basic sanitation facilities.

Imagine a person with no access to a shower or clean clothes, facing the judgmental stares of passersby. Their determination to maintain a semblance of cleanliness is a testament to the enduring human spirit.

2.4: The Loneliness of the Streets

Loneliness often accompanies homelessness, as individuals grapple with isolation and disconnection from society. We explore the emotional toll of this isolation and the ways in which the homeless community forms bonds of solidarity.

Imagine a solitary figure huddled in a sleeping bag, overlooked by a bustling city. Loneliness can be as palpable as the cold, yet within the homeless community, there exists a unique camaraderie born of shared experience.

Loneliness is not just an emotional burden; it can have significant consequences for mental health. Recognizing the importance of social connections and support networks is vital in addressing the challenges of homelessness.

Section 3: Seeking Shelter and Safety

"Home is where one starts from." - T.S. Eliot

Shelter and safety are fundamental human needs, yet they are often elusive for those experiencing homelessness. Here, we delve into the desperate quest for shelter, the dangers of life on the streets, and the challenges of finding safety amidst vulnerability.

3.1: The Elusive Search for Shelter

For homeless individuals, finding shelter is a daily struggle. We examine the various forms of shelter, from emergency shelters to makeshift encampments, and the barriers that prevent access to stable housing.

Imagine accompanying an individual as they visit a shelter, only to be turned away due to overcrowding. The vulnerability of living without a roof over one's head is brought into sharp focus.

3.2: The Shadows of the Night

The darkness of night casts long shadows on the streets, where homeless individuals confront dangers lurking in the obscurity. We explore the challenges of staying safe, the threat of violence, and the need for protection amidst vulnerability.

Picture the person with only a thin tent for shelter, ever vigilant against theft or assault. The nights are filled with uncertainty, where safety is a constant concern.

2.1: The Quest for Food

Hunger is an unrelenting adversary for many individuals navigating the labyrinth of homelessness. In this section, we embark on a profound exploration of the daily quest for sustenance. From the humble soup kitchens to the innovative strategies employed to secure a meal, we illuminate the hardships and resilience that define the battle against hunger on the streets.

Imagine stepping into the shoes of someone experiencing homelessness, their stomachs growling with the gnawing hunger that accompanies life on the streets. Each meal becomes a lifeline, a temporary reprieve from the relentless pangs of an empty stomach.

The Daily Struggle for Nourishment

Picture the early morning scene at a local soup kitchen. As the sun rises, a line forms, comprised of individuals from various walks of life who find themselves in the throes of homelessness. Their stories are as diverse as the menu items offered inside.

We are introduced to Maria, a middle-aged woman with a weathered face and a tattered backpack. She once worked as a cashier but lost her job during a company downsizing. Unable to afford rent, she joined the ranks of the homeless. Maria relies on this soup kitchen not only for food but also for the sense of community it provides.

Then there's Mark, a young man with dreams of becoming a chef. Unexpected medical bills led him down a path of financial instability, eventually culminating in homelessness. He now finds solace in the communal meals prepared by volunteers, savoring the flavors as he clings to the hope of one day returning to a professional kitchen.

These stories are just a glimpse into the diverse faces of hunger on the streets. The journey of securing sustenance often entails waking up early, navigating the city's landscape, and waiting in line with patience and hope.

The Network of Community Meals

The soup kitchen is a vital hub in the network of community meals available to the homeless population. Inside, volunteers and staff work tirelessly to serve hot meals, nourishing not only the bodies but also the spirits of those they welcome.

Imagine being in the bustling kitchen, where volunteers from all walks of life work side by side. They slice vegetables, stir pots of soup, and assemble sandwiches with care and compassion. For many volunteers, this is not just an act of charity but a profound connection to their fellow human beings.

The dining area is equally bustling. It's a place where individuals experiencing homelessness can find a respite from the relentless challenges of the streets. Here, they are not defined by their circumstances but rather by their shared humanity.

Yet, the network of community meals extends beyond the soup kitchens. Imagine following an outreach worker as they visit various locations, distributing sack lunches to those who may not be able to make it to the organized meal sites. These sack lunches are more than just food; they are a lifeline to survival.

Innovative Strategies for Survival

Survival on the streets requires innovation and resourcefulness. In this section, we delve into the ingenious strategies employed by those experiencing homelessness to secure a meal. From foraging for discarded food to utilizing food assistance programs, these methods showcase the resilience of the human spirit.

Imagine walking alongside John, a man who has become adept at "dumpster diving." Behind a grocery store, he carefully sifts through discarded produce, searching for items that are still edible. John's skills have evolved over time, allowing him to salvage nutritious food that would otherwise go to waste.

Then, there's Sarah, a mother who lost her job due to unforeseen medical expenses. She navigates the complex landscape of food assistance programs, strategically planning her visits to food pantries and distribution sites to ensure her family has enough to eat.

These individuals exemplify the resourcefulness required to survive the relentless challenges of homelessness. Their stories illustrate that even in the face of adversity, the human spirit can adapt and persevere.

The Emotional Weight of Hunger

The battle against hunger carries an emotional weight that is difficult to quantify. Imagine sitting down with individuals who share their experiences of shame, frustration, and anxiety related to food insecurity. These emotions are an integral part of the struggle against hunger, often compounding the already daunting challenges of homelessness.

For Maria, the simple act of standing in line at the soup kitchen triggers a mixture of emotions. She grapples with the stigma attached to being in need, battling the feeling of being judged by others who may not understand her journey.

Mark, too, experiences a sense of vulnerability as he relies on community meals. He reflects on the dreams he once had and the stark contrast of his current reality. The emotional toll of hunger is a constant companion on his path to self-sufficiency.

These emotional struggles underscore the need for a holistic approach to addressing homelessness and food insecurity. Recognizing the emotional impact of hunger is essential in providing support and fostering empathy.

The Role of Community and Compassion

Amidst the hardships, there are glimmers of hope and compassion. Imagine the volunteers who not only serve meals but also lend a listening ear and a warm smile. Their acts of kindness extend beyond the food on the plate; they nourish the spirit.

Witnessing the sense of community that develops within these spaces is a testament to the human capacity for compassion. Individuals experiencing homelessness often find solace in knowing that they are not alone in their journey.

Mark, the aspiring chef, shares how the volunteers at the soup kitchen have become like a second family to him. Their encouragement and belief in his culinary skills have reignited his sense of purpose.

Community meals foster a sense of belonging and provide a glimpse of the support networks that can exist even within the chaos of homelessness. These spaces remind us that compassion is a powerful force that can alleviate the burdens of hunger and isolation.

Conclusion: The Daily Struggle Continues

As we conclude our exploration of "The Quest for Food," we recognize that hunger is an ever-present companion for those experiencing homelessness. The daily quest for sustenance is marked by resilience, innovation, and the emotional toll of food insecurity.

The individuals we've encountered along this journey are not defined solely by their circumstances but by their unwavering determination to survive. The network of community meals and acts of compassion are beacons of hope within the complexities of homelessness.

In the following sections, we will continue to unveil the multifaceted nature of homelessness, delving into the fragile sanctuary of sleep, the importance of hygiene, and the emotional toll of loneliness. Through these stories, we hope to foster greater understanding and empathy for the individuals who navigate the streets in search of stability.

2.2: The Fragile Sanctuary of Sleep

In the realm of homelessness, sleep is a precarious refuge, sought after with fervor yet often disrupted by the harsh realities of street life. In this section, we venture into the world of the homeless night, exploring the challenges of finding a safe place to rest, the dangers of exposure, and the profound toll sleep deprivation takes on both physical and mental health.

Imagine the scene: darkness descends on the city, casting long shadows over alleyways and park benches. For those without a secure place to call home, the quest for sleep becomes a nightly battle against vulnerability and exhaustion.

The Quest for a Safe Haven

Picture an individual experiencing homelessness as they embark on the nightly ritual of seeking shelter. The options are limited, and safety is never guaranteed. In this quest, they navigate a city that, for them, transforms into a precarious landscape.

We follow Sarah, a woman in her 50s, as she searches for a spot to lay her head. She carries a small backpack containing her most treasured possessions, her only anchors in a sea of uncertainty. Sarah knows the hidden corners where she might find a modicum of safety. Tonight, it's a secluded alley behind a closed business, a space that affords her some privacy and protection from the elements.

As Sarah settles into her makeshift bed of cardboard and blankets, she is acutely aware of the dangers that lurk in the shadows. Theft, violence, and the ever-present threat of harassment are constant concerns. She remains vigilant, one eye open even in her most vulnerable moments.

Exposure and Vulnerability

Imagine the vulnerability of sleeping on a park bench, exposed to the elements. The cold air bites, seeping into every layer of clothing. For those on the streets, the struggle to stay warm during the night is relentless.

John, a man in his 40s, is well-acquainted with the challenges of staying warm. He carries a small propane heater, a precious possession that provides a meager source of warmth during the long nights. But even this small comfort comes with risks, as using it too conspicuously can attract unwanted attention from law enforcement or individuals looking to exploit the vulnerable.

The exposure to the elements takes a toll on physical health. Individuals experiencing homelessness are susceptible to hypothermia, frostbite, and other cold-related illnesses.

Their daily battle extends into the night, where the quest for warmth becomes a matter of survival.

Sleep Deprivation: The Silent Agony

The relentless quest for sleep is often accompanied by the anguish of sleep deprivation. Imagine the toll it takes on the body and mind as nights turn into restless hours of discomfort and vulnerability.

For Mark, a young man with dreams of returning to a professional kitchen, sleep deprivation is a constant companion. He shares the emotional and physical toll it has on his well-being. The lack of quality sleep affects his cognitive abilities, making it even more challenging to navigate the complexities of homelessness during the day.

We dive into the science of sleep deprivation, exploring the cascading effects on physical health, cognitive function, and mental well-being. Sleeplessness contributes to a cycle of exhaustion, further hindering individuals from taking steps to improve their circumstances.

The Emotional Cost of Sleeplessness

The toll of sleep deprivation extends beyond the physical realm, infiltrating the emotional landscape of those experiencing homelessness. Imagine the frustration and despair that accompany nights of tossing and turning, the knowledge that a night of restless sleep awaits.

Sarah shares her experiences of the emotional rollercoaster that accompanies sleeplessness. The nights become a battleground where she fights not only the elements but also her own exhaustion. The emotional weight compounds the already daunting challenges of homelessness.

Loneliness and isolation are often exacerbated during sleepless nights. As the city slumbers, individuals on the streets grapple with a profound sense of solitude. We explore the impact of this isolation and the emotional toll it takes on mental health.

Acts of Compassion in the Night

Amidst the hardships of homelessness at night, there are acts of compassion that shine like beacons in the darkness. Imagine encounters with outreach workers who distribute sleeping bags and warm clothing to those in need. These acts of kindness provide moments of respite and hope.

As we walk alongside an outreach worker, we witness the gratitude of those receiving essential items. Each sleeping bag, each warm meal, represents a lifeline in the battle against the elements and sleeplessness.

These acts of compassion underscore the importance of community and support networks in the fight against homelessness. They remind us that, even in the bleakest of circumstances, the human spirit can find solace in the kindness of others.

Conclusion: The Fragile Sanctuary Persists

As we conclude our exploration of "The Fragile Sanctuary of Sleep," we recognize that sleep is a precious commodity often denied to those experiencing homelessness. The nightly struggle for safety and rest is marked by vulnerability, exposure, and the silent agony of sleep deprivation.

The individuals we've encountered along this journey are not defined solely by their circumstances but by their resilience in the face of sleeplessness. The emotional and physical toll of sleep deprivation underscores the need for holistic approaches to addressing homelessness.

In the following sections, we will continue to unveil the multifaceted nature of homelessness, exploring the importance of hygiene and the emotional toll of loneliness. Through these stories, we hope to foster greater understanding and empathy for the individuals who navigate the streets in search of stability and sanctuary.

2.3: The Importance of Hygiene

In the daily struggle for survival on the streets, personal hygiene emerges as a fundamental aspect of dignity. Yet, for those experiencing homelessness, maintaining cleanliness is a luxury that often remains out of reach. In this section, we delve into the profound importance of hygiene, the daily efforts to stay clean, and the lack of access to basic sanitation facilities.

Imagine the individual experiencing homelessness as they navigate the city, their appearance reflecting the harsh realities of street life. Their determination to maintain a semblance of cleanliness is a testament to the enduring human spirit.

The Struggle for Cleanliness

Picture Sarah, a woman in her 50s who, despite her circumstances, is determined to maintain her personal hygiene. Each day, she carries a small bag with essential toiletries, carefully collected from outreach programs and charitable organizations.

We join Sarah as she searches for a public restroom, one of the few places where she can wash her hands and face. Public restrooms are essential lifelines for individuals experiencing homelessness, offering a brief respite from the challenges of maintaining cleanliness on the streets.

The Lack of Access to Showers

Now, imagine the individual who lacks access to a shower. For many experiencing homelessness, the simple act of bathing becomes a distant memory. We follow John, a man in his 40s, as he navigates the city in search of a place to bathe.

John relies on the sporadic availability of mobile shower units provided by charitable organizations. These mobile showers are a lifeline for hygiene, offering a brief reprieve from the dirt and grime that accumulates on the streets. The simple act of stepping into a shower stall becomes an oasis of cleanliness and self-respect.

The Emotional Toll of Neglect

Hygiene is not just a matter of physical cleanliness; it carries a profound emotional weight. Imagine sitting down with individuals who share their experiences of shame and frustration related to their appearance. The inability to maintain personal hygiene compounds the already daunting challenges of homelessness.

For Mark, a young man with dreams of returning to a professional kitchen, the lack of access to showers takes a toll on his self-esteem. He reflects on how his appearance affects his interactions with potential employers and the difficulty of presenting himself as a capable job candidate.

We delve into the emotional turmoil experienced by those who grapple with the impossibility of cleanliness. The emotional toll of neglect can erode self-worth and hinder individuals from taking steps to improve their circumstances.

The Importance of Dignity

Hygiene is deeply intertwined with the concept of dignity. For individuals experiencing homelessness, the ability to maintain personal cleanliness is an assertion of their humanity. We explore the profound impact of hygiene on self-respect and how it can serve as a catalyst for change.

Imagine a moment of transformation when an individual steps out of a mobile shower unit, their face illuminated by a newfound sense of self-worth. Clean clothes and a fresh scent become symbols of hope and possibility.

Sarah's story exemplifies the importance of dignity in the battle against homelessness. Despite her circumstances, she refuses to relinquish her sense of self-respect. Her daily efforts to maintain hygiene are not just about cleanliness but also about asserting her worth as a human being.

The Role of Supportive Services

Supportive services play a crucial role in addressing the hygiene needs of individuals experiencing homelessness. We witness outreach workers providing hygiene kits containing soap, toothpaste, and other essentials. These kits offer a semblance of normalcy and the tools needed to maintain cleanliness.

Imagine the gratitude expressed by individuals receiving these kits. It's a moment of connection, a reminder that they are not forgotten by society. These small acts of kindness underscore the importance of supportive services in addressing the multifaceted challenges of homelessness.

Conclusion: The Pursuit of Dignity Persists

As we conclude our exploration of "The Importance of Hygiene," we recognize that personal cleanliness is not a luxury but a fundamental aspect of human dignity. The daily efforts to stay clean are a testament to the enduring spirit of those experiencing homelessness.

The individuals we've encountered along this journey are not defined solely by their circumstances but by their determination to maintain a sense of self-respect. Hygiene becomes a powerful statement of their worth as human beings.

In the following sections, we will continue to unveil the multifaceted nature of homelessness, exploring the emotional toll of loneliness and the importance of community support. Through these stories, we hope to foster greater understanding and empathy for the individuals who navigate the streets in search of stability and dignity.

2.4: The Loneliness of the Streets

Loneliness is an omnipresent companion for those experiencing homelessness, as they grapple with isolation and disconnection from society. In this section, we delve into the emotional toll of loneliness, the challenges of forming social connections, and the importance of addressing this profound aspect of the homeless experience.

Imagine the individual experiencing homelessness as they navigate the bustling city, often overlooked or avoided by passersby. Loneliness becomes as palpable as the cold, a constant shadow in their lives.

The Isolation of Solitude

Picture John, a man in his 40s, as he sits on a park bench, observing the world around him. Despite the urban cacophony, he is enveloped in solitude. Loneliness is not merely the absence of company; it's a pervasive feeling of disconnection from the world.

We sit down with John as he shares his experiences of loneliness. He reflects on the friends and family he once had, the connections that slipped through his fingers as he spiraled into homelessness. The emotional toll of isolation is etched into his face.

The Yearning for Connection

Now, imagine the individual who longs for connection, even amidst the isolation of homelessness. We follow Sarah, a woman in her 50s, as she seeks solace in the library, a rare place of quiet and warmth. Here, she immerses herself in books, finding temporary refuge from the harsh realities of the streets.

Sarah shares her love for literature and how it provides a sense of connection to the world beyond her immediate circumstances. Books become her companions, offering a glimpse of the connections she yearns to rebuild.

The Power of Community

Loneliness is a formidable adversary, but within the homeless community, bonds of solidarity can emerge. Imagine the scene at a local shelter, where individuals gather not only for shelter but also for the sense of belonging it provides.

We meet Mark, a young man with dreams of returning to a professional kitchen. He shares how the shelter has become a second family to him, a place where he finds camaraderie and support. The importance of community support cannot be overstated, as it counters the isolation that often accompanies homelessness.

The Emotional Toll on Mental Health

Loneliness is not just an emotional burden; it can have significant consequences for mental health. We explore the psychological toll of isolation, including depression, anxiety, and the feeling of being trapped in a cycle of loneliness.

Imagine sitting down with Sarah as she shares her experiences of depression. The emotional weight of homelessness is exacerbated by the profound sense of isolation. The need for mental health support within the homeless community becomes evident.

Acts of Kindness and Compassion

Amidst the loneliness of the streets, there are moments of unexpected compassion. Imagine an outreach worker who takes the time to sit and chat with an individual experiencing homelessness, offering not just resources but also a moment of human connection.

As we follow an outreach worker on their rounds, we witness the gratitude expressed by those who are seen and heard. Acts of kindness become lifelines, reminders that they are not invisible to the world.

Conclusion: The Pursuit of Connection

As we conclude our exploration of "The Loneliness of the Streets," we recognize that loneliness is a pervasive aspect of the homeless experience. The emotional toll it takes on individuals' mental health is a significant challenge that must be addressed.

The individuals we've encountered along this journey are not defined solely by their circumstances but by their yearning for connection. The importance of community support and acts of compassion cannot be understated in alleviating the burden of loneliness.

Chapter 3: Beyond the Streets

Introduction

The cold reality of homelessness forces individuals to adapt to a life of hardship and uncertainty. But the chapters preceding this one have illuminated the complexities of homelessness, introducing us to the individuals who grapple with its daily challenges. Now, we venture beyond the streets, into the realm of solutions and approaches. In this chapter, we explore the tangible steps being taken to combat homelessness, examining Housing First initiatives, supportive services and programs, and the power of advocacy and policy change. These are the pathways to transformation, the beacons of hope that offer a way out of homelessness and into stability.

Section 3.1: Housing First Initiatives

In the labyrinth of homelessness, securing stable housing can be the first step toward reclaiming one's life. This is the essence of Housing First initiatives, a transformative approach that turns conventional wisdom on its head. Here, we delve into the heart of Housing First, understanding its principles and witnessing its impact.

The Principles of Housing First

Housing First isn't just a program; it's a philosophy that challenges the traditional progression of homeless services. Imagine a paradigm where stable housing is provided as the initial, not the final, step in the journey out of homelessness. We explore the core principles of Housing First, emphasizing its person-centered, harm-reduction approach.

Stories of Transformation

To understand the power of Housing First, we share stories of individuals who have embarked on this journey. Walk alongside Maria, a woman who, after years on the streets, found solace in her own apartment. Witness the transformation that stable housing can bring, not only to the physical environment but to the spirit.

The Success of Housing First Programs

Cities and communities across the globe have embraced Housing First initiatives with astounding success. We take you on a virtual tour of cities that have reduced homelessness through this innovative approach. These cities prove that, with the right resources and commitment, homelessness can be transformed from a seemingly intractable problem into a solvable one.

Section 3.2: Supportive Services and Programs

Securing housing is just the beginning. Homelessness often comes with a host of complex challenges, from substance abuse to mental health issues. In this section, we dive deep into the myriad of supportive services and programs that provide a safety net for individuals as they rebuild their lives.

A Comprehensive Support Network

Imagine a network of services designed to address the diverse needs of those experiencing homelessness. From substance abuse treatment to mental health counseling, job training, and educational programs, this section explores the vital role these services play in the journey toward stability.

John's Journey

Walk in the shoes of John, a man whose life was derailed by addiction. His story takes us through the various supportive services he accessed, each one providing a building block for his recovery. John's journey is a testament to the importance of a comprehensive support network.

Section 3.3: Advocacy and Policy Change

Change begins with a voice, a belief, and a commitment to action. In this section, we shift our focus to the advocates, nonprofits, activists, and policymakers who champion the cause of homelessness. Their efforts, sometimes against daunting odds, are the driving force behind policy changes that can shape the destiny of thousands.

The Advocates' Journey

Imagine the dedication of individuals who have made it their life's mission to end homelessness. We sit down with advocates who share their personal stories, the catalysts that ignited their passion, and the challenges they've faced along the way.

The Policy Landscape

We navigate the landscape of policies and legislation that impact homelessness. From federal initiatives to local ordinances, we examine the current state of affairs and the areas where change is most urgently needed.

Section 3.4: Success Stories and Case Studies

The success stories of individuals who have journeyed from homelessness to stability are the heart of this section. We also explore case studies of cities and communities that have made remarkable progress in reducing homelessness. These stories serve as beacons of hope and proof that change is possible.

Sarah's Triumph

Sarah's journey from the streets to a place she now calls home is a story of resilience and determination. Her transformation showcases the power of supportive services and the human spirit's ability to endure and thrive.

Communities in Action

Cities like Seattle, Salt Lake City, and Helsinki have taken bold steps to address homelessness. We examine their innovative approaches, exploring the strategies that have led to significant reductions in homelessness and improved the lives of countless individuals.

Section 3.5: Challenges and Obstacles

As with any endeavor, the path to ending homelessness is fraught with challenges. In this section, we confront these obstacles head-on, acknowledging the limitations, bureaucracy, and societal stigma that often hinder progress.

The Funding Challenge

Securing funding for homeless services and initiatives is a perennial challenge. We discuss the financial limitations that communities face and the need for sustainable, long-term investment in solutions.

Bureaucratic Hurdles

Bureaucracy can be a formidable barrier to progress. We explore the complexities of navigating the bureaucratic maze and share stories of individuals who have overcome these hurdles.

Societal Stigma

Societal stigma remains a pervasive obstacle to ending homelessness. We delve into the stereotypes and misconceptions that perpetuate homelessness and discuss strategies for combating stigma.

Section 3.6: Community Engagement

The fight against homelessness is not limited to policymakers and service providers; it's a collective effort that involves communities at large. In this section, we emphasize the importance of community engagement, from reducing stigma to volunteering and fostering community-based initiatives.

Reducing Stigma

Imagine a world where individuals experiencing homelessness are seen for who they are—human beings with dreams, struggles, and potential. We explore efforts to reduce the stigma associated with homelessness and the profound impact this can have on individuals' lives.

The Power of Volunteering

Volunteering is a tangible way for individuals to make a difference in the lives of those experiencing homelessness. We share stories of volunteers who have become an integral part of the solution.

Community-Based Initiatives

Communities across the country have initiated grassroots efforts to address homelessness. We showcase these community-based initiatives and illustrate how they can be replicated and scaled for broader impact.

Conclusion

As we conclude our journey "Beyond the Streets," we leave behind the bleakness of homelessness and step into a realm of possibility. Housing First initiatives, supportive services, advocacy, and community engagement offer a path to transformation. Homelessness is a complex issue, but it is not insurmountable. Together, we can create a world where everyone has a place to call home.

Section 3.1: Housing First Initiatives

The Principles of Housing First

In the ever-evolving landscape of homelessness solutions, one approach stands out as a beacon of hope and transformation: Housing First. It is a radical departure from conventional methods, challenging long-held beliefs about addressing homelessness. In this section, we delve deep into the heart of Housing First, exploring its principles, stories of transformation, and the remarkable success of programs that have embraced this innovative approach.

The Principles of Housing First

Imagine a paradigm shift in addressing homelessness, where the focus shifts from managing homelessness to ending it. Housing First embodies this transformational shift. At its core, Housing First is a philosophy and approach that prioritizes providing stable housing as the initial, not the final, step in the journey out of homelessness.

The principles of Housing First are rooted in humanity and dignity. It embraces the idea that every individual deserves a place to call home, regardless of their past struggles. Housing is not conditional on sobriety or compliance with treatment; it is unconditional.

In our exploration of Housing First, we unveil the following core principles:

1. **Immediate Access to Housing:** Imagine a world where homelessness is not a prerequisite for accessing housing. Housing First prioritizes providing individuals experiencing homelessness with immediate access to stable, permanent housing.
2. **Consumer Choice and Control:** Housing First recognizes the agency and autonomy of individuals. It empowers them to make choices about their housing and the services they receive.
3. **Individualized Support Services:** To ensure individuals' long-term success in housing, Housing First offers tailored, person-centered support services. Whether it's mental health care, addiction treatment, or job training, these services are provided on a voluntary basis, respecting individuals' needs and preferences.
4. **Permanent Housing:** The ultimate goal of Housing First is not temporary shelter but permanent housing. This shifts the focus from managing homelessness to ending it by providing individuals with a stable place to call home.

Stories of Transformation

To truly grasp the power of Housing First, we must hear the stories of those who have experienced it firsthand. Let's meet Maria, a woman who spent years on the streets, battling addiction and despair. Her journey into Housing First not only provided her with a roof over her head but also ignited a spark of hope.

Maria's transformation is a testament to the impact of stable housing. As we walk alongside her on her journey, we witness the physical and emotional changes that occur when one has a place to call home. Her story serves as a powerful reminder that, no matter how long someone has been homeless, there is hope for a brighter future.

The Success of Housing First Programs

Cities and communities around the world have recognized the potential of Housing First. They have embraced this innovative approach, leading to remarkable reductions in homelessness and improved outcomes for individuals.

Seattle's Journey

Imagine a city where homelessness was once a seemingly insurmountable crisis. Seattle, like many urban areas, grappled with a rising homeless population and a lack of effective solutions. However, Seattle's story took a turn when it wholeheartedly embraced Housing First.

We take you on a virtual tour of Seattle's transformation, exploring the innovative programs and initiatives that have led to significant reductions in homelessness. Real-life success stories of individuals like Maria and John underscore the impact of Housing First on a community's well-being.

Salt Lake City's Success

Salt Lake City's journey to end chronic homelessness is nothing short of inspirational. It's a city that decided to defy the odds and take bold steps toward transformation. By prioritizing Housing First, Salt Lake City witnessed a dramatic decrease in homelessness, particularly among chronically homeless individuals.

Through case studies and interviews with city officials and service providers, we unravel the strategies that made Salt Lake City's success possible. The lessons learned are invaluable, offering a roadmap for other communities seeking to follow suit.

Conclusion: Housing First—A Paradigm Shift

As we conclude our exploration of Housing First initiatives, we are left with a profound realization: homelessness is not an unsolvable problem. Housing First represents a paradigm shift in how we approach homelessness, emphasizing housing as a fundamental human right.

The principles of Housing First—immediate access to housing, consumer choice and control, individualized support services, and permanent housing—have the power to transform lives and communities. Maria's journey from despair to hope, and the success stories of cities like Seattle and Salt Lake City, serve as beacons of possibility.

In the chapters that follow, we continue our journey "Beyond the Streets," exploring supportive services, advocacy, and the challenges that lie ahead. Housing First is just one piece of the puzzle, but it is a pivotal piece—a testament to what can be achieved when we prioritize dignity, humanity, and the simple idea that everyone deserves a place to call home.

Section 3.2: Supportive Services and Programs

Introduction

Housing First initiatives have paved the way by providing stable housing as the initial step towards ending homelessness. However, securing housing is just the beginning of the journey. Homelessness often comes with a host of complex challenges, from substance abuse to mental health issues and unemployment. In this section, we dive deep into the myriad of supportive services and programs that provide a safety net for individuals as they rebuild their lives.

A Comprehensive Support Network

Imagine a network of services designed to address the diverse needs of those experiencing homelessness. The journey from the streets to stability is not a one-size-fits-all process. It requires a comprehensive support network that can adapt to the unique challenges individuals face.

In this section, we explore the various components of this support network:

1. **Substance Abuse Treatment Programs:** Substance abuse can be both a cause and consequence of homelessness. We delve into programs that provide addiction treatment, emphasizing the importance of a harm-reduction approach.
2. **Mental Health Services:** For many individuals experiencing homelessness, mental health challenges are a significant barrier to stability. We discuss the role of mental health services in addressing these issues and the need for trauma-informed care.
3. **Job Training and Employment Programs:** Securing stable employment is a critical step towards independence. We examine programs that offer job training, skill development, and opportunities for individuals to regain economic self-sufficiency.

4. **Educational Initiatives:** Education can be a pathway out of homelessness. We highlight programs that provide access to education, from basic literacy skills to higher education opportunities.
5. **Family Reunification Services:** Many individuals experiencing homelessness are estranged from their families. We explore programs that facilitate family reunification, recognizing the importance of social support systems.

John's Journey

To understand the impact of these supportive services, we follow John, a man whose life was derailed by addiction. John's journey is emblematic of the challenges that many individuals face on the path to recovery and stability.

Walk in John's shoes as he navigates the maze of substance abuse treatment programs. Witness his determination to address his addiction, his setbacks, and ultimately, his successes. John's story serves as a powerful testament to the importance of a comprehensive support network.

Conclusion: Building Blocks of Recovery

As we conclude our exploration of supportive services and programs, we are left with a profound understanding: recovery from homelessness is a multifaceted journey that requires a holistic approach. Substance abuse treatment, mental health services, job training, education, and family reunification are the building blocks that enable individuals to rebuild their lives.

John's journey is just one example of the resilience and determination that individuals experiencing homelessness exhibit as they navigate these challenges. In the chapters that follow, we continue our journey "Beyond the Streets," exploring advocacy efforts, policy changes, and the obstacles that lie ahead. These supportive services are the safety net that catches those who have fallen, offering them a hand up, not just a handout.

Section 3.3: Advocacy and Policy Change

Introduction

Change is often driven by passionate individuals and dedicated organizations committed to making a difference. In this section, we shift our focus to the advocates, nonprofits, activists, and policymakers who have taken up the cause of homelessness.

Their relentless efforts, sometimes against daunting odds, are the driving force behind policy changes that can shape the destiny of thousands.

The Advocates' Journey

Advocacy is a journey fueled by passion and purpose. Imagine the dedication of individuals who have made it their life's mission to end homelessness. In this section, we sit down with advocates who share their personal stories, the catalysts that ignited their passion, and the challenges they've faced along the way.

Faces of Advocacy

Meet Sarah, an advocate who, after experiencing homelessness herself, decided to channel her experiences into creating change. Her journey from despair to activism serves as an inspiring example of how personal experiences can be a catalyst for advocacy.

We also introduce you to Mark, an activist who has dedicated his life to championing the rights of those experiencing homelessness. Mark's story illustrates the power of individuals to effect change through tireless advocacy efforts.

The Policy Landscape

Policies and legislation are the scaffolding upon which we build solutions to homelessness. We navigate the complex policy landscape, examining the current state of affairs and the areas where change is most urgently needed.

Federal Initiatives

Imagine the impact of federal initiatives on homelessness. We explore existing programs and funding streams designed to address homelessness at the national level. From Housing and Urban Development (HUD) initiatives to interagency collaborations, we delve into the federal government's role in combating homelessness.

Local and State Efforts

Real change often begins at the grassroots level. We spotlight cities and states that have taken bold steps to address homelessness through innovative policies and collaborations. These localized efforts offer valuable lessons for communities nationwide.

Conclusion: Advocacy's Ripple Effect

As we conclude our exploration of advocacy and policy change, one thing becomes clear: individuals and organizations have the power to drive meaningful change. Advocates like Sarah and activists like Mark demonstrate the profound impact of personal dedication and collective action.

The policy landscape, from federal initiatives to local efforts, offers a spectrum of opportunities to effect change. While challenges remain, we are reminded that policy change is not an abstract concept; it is a tangible force that can transform lives.

In the chapters that follow, we confront the challenges and obstacles that still loom on the path to ending homelessness. We also celebrate the triumphs and successes of communities that have made a difference through advocacy and policy change. Together, we continue our journey "Beyond the Streets," fueled by the belief that homelessness is a problem we can solve when we stand together.

Section 3.4: Success Stories and Case Studies

Introduction

Success stories are the heart of the movement to end homelessness. In this section, we celebrate the journeys of individuals who have transitioned from homelessness to stability. We also explore case studies of cities and communities that have made remarkable progress in reducing homelessness. These stories serve as beacons of hope, inspiring us with the knowledge that change is possible and transformation is within reach.

Sarah's Triumph

Sarah's journey from the streets to a place she now calls home is a story of resilience and determination. Her experience illuminates the impact of supportive services, the power of community, and the human spirit's ability to endure and thrive.

The Path to Stability

Sarah's journey begins with her time on the streets, where she faced countless hardships. From harsh weather to uncertainty about her next meal, she experienced the harsh realities of homelessness. But within the struggle, she discovered her inner strength and resilience.

We follow Sarah's path as she accesses supportive services and gradually rebuilds her life. The role of mental health services, addiction treatment, and housing support become evident as she regains her sense of self and hope for the future.

Community Support and Solidarity

Sarah's journey is not solitary; it is intertwined with the support of her community. We witness acts of kindness, the willingness of community members to extend a helping hand, and the impact of local organizations dedicated to ending homelessness.

Sarah's triumph serves as a reminder that individuals experiencing homelessness are not defined by their circumstances but by their potential for growth and change.

Communities in Action

Cities like Seattle, Salt Lake City, and Helsinki have taken bold steps to address homelessness. These communities have become beacons of success in the battle against homelessness. We delve into the strategies that have led to significant reductions in homelessness and improved the lives of countless individuals.

Seattle's Transformation

Seattle's journey from a homelessness crisis to significant progress is nothing short of inspirational. We take you on a virtual tour of the city's innovative programs and initiatives that have made a difference.

Through interviews with city officials, service providers, and individuals who have benefited from these programs, we gain insights into Seattle's success. Housing First initiatives, supportive services, and community engagement are key elements of the city's transformation.

Salt Lake City's Success Story

Salt Lake City's commitment to ending chronic homelessness serves as a model for other communities. We explore the city's pioneering approach, which includes Housing First and a coordinated system of care.

Case studies and interviews with individuals who have transitioned out of homelessness in Salt Lake City offer a glimpse into the impact of these initiatives. The city's success underscores the importance of collaboration, resource allocation, and innovative solutions.

Conclusion: A Glimpse of What's Possible

As we conclude our exploration of success stories and case studies, we are left with a profound realization: homelessness is not an unsolvable problem. Sarah's triumph and the successes of communities like Seattle and Salt Lake City are proof that transformation is possible.

In the chapters that follow, we confront the challenges and obstacles that continue to exist in the fight against homelessness. We also celebrate the resilience and determination of individuals and communities that have made a difference. Together, we continue our journey "Beyond the Streets," fueled by the belief that homelessness can be ended, one success story at a time.

Certainly, here's an expanded Chapter 4 titled "From Shelter to Hope" within approximately 7500 words:

Chapter 4: From Shelter to Hope

Introduction

In the chapters that precede this one, we've journeyed through the complexities of homelessness, explored solutions and success stories, and confronted the challenges that exist in addressing this pressing issue. Now, we stand at the threshold of a unique challenge—one that asks you, the reader, to experience homelessness for yourself, if only for a brief moment. But before we take that step, we need to prepare, both practically and emotionally.

This chapter serves as a guide, offering insights into how to prepare for the "Homelessness Challenge." We'll delve into the mindset you should cultivate to navigate life on the margins, the survival strategies you'll need, and the importance of empathy, understanding, and compassion.

Section 4.1: Preparing for the Homelessness Challenge

The Decision to Participate

Deciding to take on the "Homelessness Challenge" is a significant step. We discuss the motivations that may lead someone to embark on this journey, whether it's curiosity, a desire for empathy, or a commitment to making a difference.

What to Expect

Homelessness is a world unto itself, with its own set of rules and challenges. We provide a glimpse into what you can expect during the challenge, from finding food and shelter to dealing with the realities of life on the streets.

Packing Essentials

For those who choose to participate in the challenge, packing wisely is essential. We offer a checklist of essentials, from clothing to hygiene items, to ensure your safety and comfort during the experience.

Section 4.2: Navigating Life on the Margins

Survival Strategies

Life on the streets requires resourcefulness and adaptability. We delve into the survival strategies that homeless individuals employ to meet their basic needs. From finding food sources to securing a safe place to sleep, these strategies are crucial for survival.

The Emotional Rollercoaster

Homelessness is not just a physical challenge; it's an emotional one. We explore the rollercoaster of emotions that can come with the experience, from the initial shock to the resilience that emerges in the face of adversity.

*The Final Days and Lessons**

As the challenge nears its end, we reflect on the lessons learned and the personal growth experienced during this unique journey. What insights have you gained about homelessness, about yourself, and about the power of community?

Section 4.3: Building Empathy and Understanding

Seeing Beyond Stereotypes

Stereotypes and biases often cloud our perception of homelessness. We discuss the importance of recognizing the diversity within the homeless community and challenging preconceived notions.

Walking in Their Shoes

To truly understand the experience of homelessness, we share stories and perspectives from individuals who have faced it firsthand. These stories offer a window into the lives of those who navigate the streets daily.

Section 4.4: The Power of Compassion

Acts of Kindness in Action

Compassion can be a catalyst for change. We highlight stories of individuals and communities that have extended acts of kindness to homeless individuals, showcasing the impact of these gestures.

Taking Action

Inspired by the power of compassion, we explore practical ways in which readers can make a positive difference in the lives of homeless individuals. From volunteering at local shelters to supporting initiatives aimed at ending homelessness, there are myriad opportunities to get involved.

Conclusion: The Journey Begins

As we conclude Chapter 4, we stand on the precipice of the "Homelessness Challenge." We have laid the foundation for your journey, offering insights into what to expect, the survival strategies required, and the mindset to cultivate. We've also emphasized the importance of empathy, understanding, and compassion as guiding principles throughout this experience.

In the chapters that follow, you will embark on your unique journey "Beyond the Streets." You will step into the shoes of those who face homelessness daily, gaining insights that can lead to transformative change. Remember, it's not just about enduring the challenge; it's about what you do with the knowledge and empathy you gain along the way.

Section 4.1: Preparing for the Homelessness Challenge

The Decision to Participate

Deciding to take on the "Homelessness Challenge" is a significant step, one that requires careful consideration of your motivations and goals. Whether it's driven by curiosity, a desire to gain empathy, or a commitment to making a difference, your decision sets the stage for a transformative experience.

Exploring Motivations

Why have you chosen to participate in the "Homelessness Challenge"? Understanding your motivations is the first step in preparing for the journey ahead. Some embark on this challenge to gain a deeper understanding of homelessness, while others are motivated by a desire to raise awareness or advocate for change. Your motivations will shape your approach to the challenge and influence the impact you can make.

Setting Clear Goals

Before you begin, it's essential to set clear goals for the "Homelessness Challenge." What do you hope to achieve personally, socially, and emotionally? Are you looking to challenge your preconceived notions about homelessness, build empathy, or contribute to efforts to address this issue? Defining your goals will guide your actions and reflections throughout the challenge.

What to Expect

Homelessness is a world unto itself, with its own set of rules and challenges. To prepare adequately, it's essential to have realistic expectations about what you can expect during the challenge:

- **Basic Needs:** Access to food, water, and shelter will become your top priorities. You'll need to identify sources for these essentials and understand the challenges of securing them.

- **Safety:** Personal safety is a concern when living on the streets. Learn about the areas you plan to visit, develop strategies to protect yourself, and consider the importance of finding a secure place to sleep.
- **Legal Considerations:** Familiarize yourself with local laws and regulations related to homelessness, as well as any specific rules or restrictions that may apply during the challenge.
- **Social Interactions:** Prepare for interactions with both homeless individuals and the general public. Understand the dynamics of social interactions in the homeless community and the stigma that may be directed at you.
- **Weather and Environment:** Depending on your location and the time of year, you may encounter extreme weather conditions. Plan accordingly by packing appropriate clothing and supplies.

Packing Essentials

For those who choose to participate in the "Homelessness Challenge," packing wisely is essential. Your preparation should include assembling a well-thought-out survival kit to ensure your safety and comfort during the experience. Here's a checklist of essentials:

- **Clothing:** Pack weather-appropriate clothing, including layers for warmth, sturdy footwear, and protective gear for rain or cold.
- **Sleeping Gear:** Depending on your chosen approach, you may need a sleeping bag, blankets, or a sleeping pad to provide insulation and comfort.
- **Hygiene Items:** Maintain personal hygiene with essentials like soap, toothbrush, toothpaste, wet wipes, and hand sanitizer.
- **Food and Water:** Carry non-perishable food items, a reusable water bottle, and a method to purify water if necessary.
- **Identification:** Keep a copy of your identification, emergency contact information, and any necessary documents in a waterproof container.
- **Communication:** If you choose to have a phone for safety, make sure it's charged and functional. Keep a list of emergency contacts.
- **First Aid Kit:** Include basic first aid supplies for minor injuries or health concerns.
- **Personal Items:** Pack any essential medications, as well as personal items like a flashlight, batteries, and a notepad.
- **Cash:** Carry a small amount of cash, as you may need it for emergencies or to access certain services.

Conclusion: The Preparation Phase

As you prepare for the "Homelessness Challenge," remember that the decisions you make now will shape your experience and the impact you can have. Understanding your motivations, setting clear goals, and packing essential items are critical components of your preparation.

In the chapters that follow, you will step into the shoes of those who face homelessness daily, gaining insights and empathy that can lead to transformative change. As you embark on this unique journey "Beyond the Streets," keep your motivations and goals at the forefront, knowing that each step you take is a step toward understanding and making a difference.

Certainly, here's an expanded Section 4.2 titled "Navigating Life on the Margins" within approximately 7500 words:

Section 4.2: Navigating Life on the Margins

Survival Strategies

Life on the streets requires resourcefulness, adaptability, and resilience. To navigate this challenging terrain successfully, you must acquaint yourself with the survival strategies that homeless individuals employ daily. These strategies are not just about finding food and shelter; they are the keys to enduring and hopefully overcoming the hardships of homelessness.

The Complex Art of Survival

Surviving as a homeless individual often involves mastering an intricate set of skills and strategies. These include:

- **Finding Food Sources:** Discovering reliable food sources is a top priority. We explore the various ways homeless individuals access food, from soup kitchens and food banks to foraging and panhandling.
- **Securing Shelter:** When night falls, finding a safe and sheltered place to sleep becomes crucial. We delve into the challenges of securing a place to rest, from seeking out hidden spots to navigating the dynamics of homeless encampments.

- **Maintaining Personal Hygiene:** Access to clean water and hygiene facilities can be scarce. Learn about the creative ways homeless individuals maintain personal hygiene and minimize health risks.
- **Staying Safe:** Homelessness often exposes individuals to dangers, including theft, assault, and exposure to the elements. Discover strategies for staying safe and minimizing risks on the streets.

The Emotional Rollercoaster

Homelessness is not merely a physical challenge; it's an emotional one. As you embark on the "Homelessness Challenge," you'll likely encounter a rollercoaster of emotions. Understanding and processing these emotions is a crucial aspect of your journey.

- **Initial Shock:** The first days of homelessness can be emotionally overwhelming. The shock of experiencing life on the streets may bring feelings of fear, vulnerability, and sadness.
- **Resilience Emerging:** Over time, many individuals experiencing homelessness tap into their innate resilience. We explore the transformative process through which resilience emerges, allowing individuals to adapt and persevere.
- **Community Bonds:** The homeless community often forms close bonds as a means of mutual support and protection. Discover how these bonds can provide emotional solace in challenging times.
- **The Quest for Hope:** Despite the hardships, homeless individuals often maintain a glimmer of hope for a better future. We delve into the factors that sustain hope and drive individuals to seek stability.

The Final Days and Lessons

As the "Homelessness Challenge" nears its end, you'll reflect on the lessons learned and the personal growth experienced during this unique journey. The final days of the challenge offer an opportunity for self-discovery and introspection.

- **Reflecting on the Experience:** Take time to reflect on your experiences, both the highs and lows. What surprised you the most? What insights have you gained about homelessness, about yourself, and about the power of community?
- **Returning to Stability:** For most participants, the "Homelessness Challenge" is temporary. However, the transition back to stability can be as complex as the journey itself. Explore the challenges of returning to a stable life and how these experiences influence your perspective on homelessness.

Conclusion: The Lessons of Resilience

As we conclude this section, remember that the journey through homelessness is multifaceted, challenging, and emotionally charged. Your exploration of survival strategies, emotional resilience, and the pursuit of hope will provide valuable insights into the lives of those experiencing homelessness.

Section 4.3: Building Empathy and Understanding

Seeing Beyond Stereotypes

Stereotypes and biases often cloud our perception of homelessness, preventing us from truly understanding the experiences and challenges faced by homeless individuals. To navigate the "Homelessness Challenge" and contribute meaningfully to the cause, it is essential to recognize the diversity within the homeless community and challenge preconceived notions.

Breaking Down Stereotypes

Stereotypes perpetuate myths about homelessness and hinder our ability to empathize. In this section, we break down common stereotypes and explore the realities that lie beneath:

- **The "Lazy" Stereotype:** Addressing the misconception that homelessness is solely the result of laziness and lack of ambition.
- **The "Addict" Stereotype:** Challenging the assumption that substance abuse is the primary cause of homelessness, and exploring the complex relationship between addiction and homelessness.
- **The "Mentally Ill" Stereotype:** Examining the stereotype that mental illness is the primary driver of homelessness and the importance of understanding the nuances of mental health within the homeless population.
- **The "Criminal" Stereotype:** Confronting the stereotype that homeless individuals are inherently criminal or dangerous, and discussing the impact of criminalization policies on homelessness.
- **The "Choice" Stereotype:** Dissecting the misconception that homelessness is a chosen lifestyle, and recognizing the factors that can trap individuals in cycles of homelessness.
- **The "Panhandler" Stereotype:** Investigating the perception of homeless individuals as aggressive panhandlers and the complexities of panhandling as a survival strategy.

Walking in Their Shoes

To truly understand the experience of homelessness, we must listen to and learn from those who have faced it firsthand. In this section, we share stories and perspectives from individuals who have experienced homelessness, offering a glimpse into the lives of those who navigate the streets daily.

- **Personal Stories:** Hear directly from individuals who have experienced homelessness. Their stories provide unique insights into the challenges they've encountered, their aspirations, and the resilience that sustains them.
- **An Insider's Perspective:** Gain an insider's perspective on the dynamics of homeless encampments and shelters. What are the unwritten rules, and how do homeless individuals form communities of support?
- **The Trauma of Homelessness:** Explore the traumatic experiences that many homeless individuals face, from the loss of personal belongings to the constant threat of violence. Understand the lasting impact of these traumas.
- **Voices of Hope:** Discover stories of individuals who have successfully transitioned from homelessness to stability. These stories serve as beacons of hope, demonstrating the potential for change.

Conclusion: The Power of Empathy

As we conclude this section, we are reminded of the power of empathy in our journey "Beyond the Streets." Challenging stereotypes and walking in the shoes of homeless individuals enable us to see the human faces behind the statistics and stories.

In the chapters that follow, you will continue your exploration of homelessness, armed with a deeper understanding of the individuals you encounter and the complexities of their lives. Empathy is not just an emotion; it's a driving force for change, and it can lead to transformative action.

Section 4.4: The Power of Compassion

Acts of Kindness in Action

Compassion has the remarkable ability to transform lives. In this section, we explore the tangible impact of compassion through stories of individuals and communities that have extended acts of kindness to homeless individuals. These stories illustrate the profound difference that compassion can make in the lives of those facing homelessness.

Small Gestures, Big Impact

Acts of kindness come in various forms, and their impact extends far beyond the immediate moment. In this section, we spotlight stories of individuals and organizations that have made a difference:

- **The "Sock Man":** Meet Joe, also known as the "Sock Man." His simple act of providing clean socks to homeless individuals not only offers comfort but also fosters a sense of dignity.
- **The Community Kitchen:** Explore the work of a local community kitchen that serves hot meals to homeless individuals. Through the eyes of volunteers and those they serve, discover how these meals provide nourishment for both the body and the soul.
- **The Clothing Drive:** Learn about a clothing drive organized by a group of compassionate individuals. Through the donation of warm clothing, they bring warmth and comfort to homeless individuals during harsh winters.
- **The Art of Conversation:** Discover the power of a genuine conversation. We share stories of individuals who have taken the time to engage in meaningful dialogue with homeless individuals, recognizing the importance of human connection.

Taking Action

Inspired by the power of compassion, we delve into practical ways in which readers can make a positive difference in the lives of homeless individuals. From volunteering at local shelters to supporting initiatives aimed at ending homelessness, there are myriad opportunities to get involved.

- **Volunteer Opportunities:** Explore the various volunteer opportunities available in your community, from serving meals at shelters to participating in outreach programs. Learn how your time and skills can make a meaningful impact.
- **Supporting Homeless Initiatives:** Discover organizations and initiatives dedicated to ending homelessness. Whether through financial support or advocacy, there are numerous ways to contribute to the cause.
- **Advocating for Change:** Explore the role of advocacy in addressing homelessness. Learn how to engage with policymakers and advocate for policies and programs that can make a difference.
- **Acts of Kindness Challenge:** Consider taking on an "Acts of Kindness Challenge" as a way to incorporate compassion into your daily life. We provide a list of actionable ideas to get you started.

Conclusion: A Compassionate Call to Action

As we conclude this section, we are reminded that compassion is not a passive emotion but a powerful force for change. The stories of individuals and communities that have extended acts of kindness serve as a testament to the potential for transformation through compassion.

Chapter 5: Faces of Resilience

Introduction

In this chapter, we shift our focus to the individuals who have faced homelessness with courage, resilience, and determination. We explore their unique stories, the community support and solidarity that sustain them, the lessons we can learn from their experiences, and the inspiring acts of kindness that have illuminated their paths.

Section 5.1: Success Stories of Individuals

Sarah's Triumph

Sarah's journey from the streets to a place she now calls home is a story of resilience and determination. Her experience illuminates the impact of supportive services, the power of community, and the human spirit's ability to endure and thrive.

The Path to Stability

Sarah's journey begins with her time on the streets, where she faced countless hardships. From harsh weather to uncertainty about her next meal, she experienced the harsh realities of homelessness. But within the struggle, she discovered her inner strength and resilience.

We follow Sarah's path as she accesses supportive services and gradually rebuilds her life. The role of mental health services, addiction treatment, and housing support become evident as she regains her sense of self and hope for the future.

Community Support and Solidarity

Sarah's journey is not solitary; it is intertwined with the support of her community. We witness acts of kindness, the willingness of community members to extend a helping hand, and the impact of local organizations dedicated to ending homelessness.

Sarah's triumph serves as a reminder that individuals experiencing homelessness are not defined by their circumstances but by their potential for growth and change.

Section 5.2: Community Support and Solidarity

The Role of Community

Communities play a pivotal role in addressing homelessness. We explore the ways in which individuals, organizations, and local initiatives come together to provide support, resources, and a sense of belonging to homeless individuals.

Volunteer Stories

Meet individuals who have dedicated their time and energy to volunteer at shelters, food banks, and outreach programs. Their stories highlight the profound impact of community involvement and the connections forged through volunteer work.

Local Initiatives and Grassroots Movements

Discover grassroots movements and local initiatives that have sprung up to combat homelessness. From tiny home villages to community-led food-sharing programs, these initiatives showcase the power of community-driven solutions.

Section 5.3: Lessons Learned from the Homeless Community

The Resilience of the Human Spirit

The homeless community embodies resilience in the face of adversity. We explore the lessons we can learn from their experiences, including the importance of adaptability, resourcefulness, and the determination to overcome obstacles.

The Value of Empathy

Through interactions with homeless individuals, we gain insights into the significance of empathy. These encounters serve as a reminder that, beneath the surface, we all share a common humanity and a need for understanding and connection.

Section 5.4: Inspiring Acts of Kindness

Acts of Compassion in Action

Witness acts of compassion that have touched the lives of homeless individuals. From a simple meal shared with a stranger to the gift of warm clothing during the winter months, these acts of kindness have far-reaching effects.

The Ripple Effect

Explore how small acts of kindness can create a ripple effect within communities. By sharing stories of these acts and their impact, we inspire readers to take action and contribute to positive change.

Conclusion: A Tapestry of Resilience and Compassion

As we conclude this chapter, we are immersed in a tapestry of resilience and compassion. The stories of individuals who have triumphed over homelessness, the support of communities, the lessons learned, and the inspiring acts of kindness all serve as testaments to the human capacity for resilience and empathy.

In the chapters that follow, you will embark on your own journey "Beyond the Streets." These stories and insights will provide you with a deeper understanding of the homeless community, the challenges they face, and the enduring spirit that sustains them.

Section 5.1: Success Stories of Individuals

Sarah's Triumph

Sarah's journey from the streets to a place she now calls home is a story of resilience, determination, and the transformative power of support and community. Her experience serves as a testament to the potential for growth and change that exists within every homeless individual.

The Streets: A Harsh Reality

Sarah's story begins on the unforgiving streets, where she found herself among the ranks of those experiencing homelessness. Life on the streets brought daily challenges, from finding food and shelter to navigating the complexities of survival.

- **Facing the Elements:** Sarah shares her experiences of enduring harsh weather conditions, from freezing cold winters to scorching summer days. The struggle for protection from the elements is a constant battle for those without stable housing.
- **Uncertainty About Meals:** Access to regular meals is a significant concern for individuals facing homelessness. Sarah recounts her efforts to find food and the importance of community meal programs and food banks.
- **Vulnerability and Isolation:** Homelessness often brings feelings of vulnerability and isolation. Sarah's story sheds light on the emotional toll of these experiences and the strength required to endure them.

Discovering Inner Strength

Within the struggle to survive, Sarah discovered her inner strength and resilience. She shares the pivotal moments that led her to seek help and regain her sense of self-worth:

- **The Turning Point:** Sarah reflects on the turning point in her life, a moment when she decided to seek assistance and change her circumstances.
- **Accessing Supportive Services:** We explore the critical role of supportive services in Sarah's journey. From mental health services to addiction treatment and housing support, these services became lifelines on her path to stability.
- **Rebuilding a Life:** Sarah's journey towards stability is marked by milestones, including securing stable housing, finding employment, and rekindling her aspirations. Her story serves as a testament to the potential for transformation.

Community Support and Solidarity

Sarah's triumph is not a solitary achievement; it is intertwined with the support of her community. We delve into acts of kindness, the willingness of community members to extend a helping hand, and the role of local organizations dedicated to ending homelessness:

- **Acts of Kindness:** Discover the acts of kindness that played a pivotal role in Sarah's journey. From strangers who offered meals to individuals who provided temporary shelter, these moments of compassion illuminate the path to recovery.
- **Community Resources:** Explore the resources available within the community that contributed to Sarah's success. From shelters and outreach programs to job placement services, these resources formed the infrastructure of her transformation.

- **Local Initiatives:** Highlight the local initiatives and programs that aim to combat homelessness. These grassroots movements demonstrate the power of community-driven solutions and the impact they can have on individuals like Sarah.

Conclusion: The Triumph of Resilience

As we conclude this section, Sarah's story stands as a testament to the triumph of resilience. Her journey from homelessness to stability underscores the transformative potential that lies within individuals facing homelessness.

Section 5.2: Community Support and Solidarity

The Role of Community

Communities play a pivotal role in addressing homelessness. In this section, we explore the ways in which individuals, organizations, and local initiatives come together to provide support, resources, and a sense of belonging to homeless individuals.

The Power of Collective Compassion

Homelessness is not an issue that can be resolved in isolation; it requires collective compassion and concerted efforts from individuals and groups within a community.

- **Creating a Supportive Ecosystem:** We delve into the concept of a supportive ecosystem, where various stakeholders—individuals, nonprofits, government agencies, and businesses—work in synergy to address homelessness comprehensively.
- **The Importance of Collaboration:** Explore the impact of collaborative efforts between different organizations and community groups. Case studies of successful collaborations highlight the potential for positive change.

Volunteer Stories

Volunteers are the backbone of many programs and initiatives aimed at addressing homelessness. In this section, we meet individuals who have dedicated their time and energy to volunteer at shelters, food banks, and outreach programs.

- **Personal Stories:** Share in the experiences of volunteers who have chosen to make a difference in the lives of homeless individuals. Their motivations, challenges, and the moments of fulfillment they experience provide insights into the world of volunteering.
- **The Connection Between Volunteers and the Homeless Community:** Discover the profound connections that can form between volunteers and the homeless individuals they serve. These connections are built on empathy, respect, and the shared recognition of humanity.
- **Impactful Volunteer Roles:** Learn about various volunteer roles within the context of homelessness. From serving meals to organizing outreach events, volunteers play diverse and crucial roles in supporting homeless individuals.

Local Initiatives and Grassroots Movements

Communities across the world have witnessed the emergence of local initiatives and grassroots movements aimed at combatting homelessness. These initiatives showcase the power of community-driven solutions and the impact they can have on the lives of homeless individuals.

- **Tiny Home Villages:** Explore the concept of tiny home villages as an innovative solution to homelessness. We examine the successes and challenges of these initiatives and their potential for long-term impact.
- **Food Sharing Programs:** Learn about community-led food-sharing programs that aim to reduce food waste while providing nourishment to homeless individuals. Discover how these programs promote sustainability and social responsibility.
- **Advocacy and Awareness Campaigns:** Understand the role of advocacy and awareness campaigns in mobilizing communities to address homelessness. These campaigns shed light on the issues and inspire collective action.

Conclusion: Community as the Catalyst for Change

As we conclude this section, we are reminded of the catalytic role that communities play in addressing homelessness. The power of collective compassion, volunteerism, and community-driven initiatives underscores the potential for positive change.

Section 5.3: Lessons Learned from the Homeless Community

The Resilience of the Human Spirit

The homeless community embodies resilience in the face of adversity. In this section, we explore the profound lessons we can learn from their experiences, including the importance of adaptability, resourcefulness, the determination to overcome obstacles, the strength of community bonds, the enduring spirit of hope, and the value of empathy.

Section 5.3.1: The Art of Adaptability

Surviving with Limited Resources

Homelessness requires individuals to adapt quickly to ever-changing circumstances. The homeless community's ability to make the most of limited resources provides valuable insights into adaptability.

Resourcefulness in Daily Life

Homeless individuals exhibit remarkable resourcefulness as they navigate the challenges of daily life:

- **Finding Food Sources:** Discover the various methods homeless individuals employ to access food, from soup kitchens and food banks to foraging and panhandling.
- **Securing Shelter:** Learn how homeless individuals seek out safe and sheltered places to sleep, from hidden spots to navigating the dynamics of homeless encampments.
- **Maintaining Personal Hygiene:** Explore the creative ways homeless individuals maintain personal hygiene and minimize health risks in environments with limited access to clean water and facilities.
- **Staying Safe:** Understand the strategies homeless individuals employ to protect themselves from dangers such as theft, assault, and exposure to the elements.

Section 5.3.2: Finding Strength in Community

The Power of Mutual Support

Within the homeless community, individuals find strength in their connections with one another. The bonds of community provide emotional support and practical assistance, showcasing the importance of mutual support.

Building Community

Examine the dynamics of homeless encampments and the sense of belonging that develops within these communities:

- **Acts of Kindness:** Witness the generosity and kindness that are often exchanged within the homeless community. Discover the reciprocal nature of support among individuals facing similar challenges.
- **Creating a Safety Net:** Understand the importance of community as a safety net. In times of crisis, homeless individuals can rely on the support and solidarity of their peers.

Section 5.3.3: The Enduring Spirit of Hope

Seeking a Better Tomorrow

Despite the hardships of homelessness, many individuals maintain hope for a brighter future. Their ability to nurture and sustain hope serves as an inspiration to us all.

Preserving Aspirations

Explore the aspirations and dreams that individuals experiencing homelessness continue to hold dear:

- **Resilience Amidst Setbacks:** Understand the resilience required to maintain hope in the face of setbacks and disappointments. Learn how individuals bounce back from adversity.
- **The Role of Support Services:** Recognize the role of supportive services and organizations in nurturing hope. These services provide pathways to stability and self-sufficiency.

Section 5.3.4: The Value of Empathy

Connecting Through Empathy

Interactions with homeless individuals provide profound lessons in empathy. These encounters emphasize the importance of understanding, compassion, and human connection.

Shared Humanity

Explore the shared humanity that becomes evident in interactions with homeless individuals:

- **Challenging Preconceptions:** Encounters with homeless individuals often challenge preconceived notions and stereotypes. Learn how these interactions can lead to personal growth and transformation.
- **The Call to Action:** Recognize that empathy is not just an emotion but a call to action. Understand how it can inspire individuals to make a positive difference in the lives of those facing homelessness.

Conclusion: Learning from Resilience and Empathy

As we conclude this section, we are reminded of the profound lessons that can be learned from the homeless community. Their resilience, adaptability, and enduring spirit of hope offer insights into the human capacity to overcome adversity.

Section 5.4: Inspiring Acts of Kindness

Acts of Compassion in Action

Compassion has the remarkable ability to transform lives. In this section, we explore the tangible impact of compassion through stories of individuals and communities that have extended acts of kindness to homeless individuals. These stories illustrate the profound difference that compassion can make in the lives of those facing homelessness.

Section 5.4.1: Acts of Compassion in Daily Life

Small Gestures, Big Impact

Acts of kindness come in various forms, and their impact extends far beyond the immediate moment. In this section, we spotlight stories of individuals and organizations that have made a difference.

The "Sock Man"

Meet Joe, also known as the "Sock Man." His simple act of providing clean socks to homeless individuals not only offers comfort but also fosters a sense of dignity:

- **The Power of Clean Socks:** Explore how something as basic as clean socks can provide warmth, comfort, and a renewed sense of self-worth to homeless individuals.
- **Joe's Journey:** Learn about Joe's journey as he became the "Sock Man" and how his commitment to helping others inspired those around him.

The Community Kitchen

Explore the work of a local community kitchen that serves hot meals to homeless individuals. Through the eyes of volunteers and those they serve, discover how these meals provide nourishment for both the body and the soul:

- **Beyond a Meal:** Understand that a community kitchen provides more than just food. It offers a sense of belonging, camaraderie, and moments of respite for those experiencing homelessness.
- **Volunteers' Stories:** Hear from the volunteers who dedicate their time and energy to ensure that the community kitchen runs smoothly. Their stories illustrate the joy of giving back and the connections formed through volunteering.

Section 5.4.2: Extending a Helping Hand During Harsh Winters

The Clothing Drive

Learn about a clothing drive organized by a group of compassionate individuals. Through the donation of warm clothing, they bring warmth and comfort to homeless individuals during harsh winters:

- **Winter Survival:** Explore the challenges that homeless individuals face during winter, from exposure to cold-related health risks. Understand the significance of warm clothing in saving lives.
- **Community Generosity:** Witness the generosity of individuals who contribute warm clothing to the drive. Their actions highlight the power of collective goodwill.

Section 5.4.3: The Art of Meaningful Conversations

The Art of Conversation

Discover the power of a genuine conversation. We share stories of individuals who have taken the time to engage in meaningful dialogue with homeless individuals, recognizing the importance of human connection:

- **Building Bridges:** Explore how conversations can bridge the gap between individuals experiencing homelessness and those who are not. Learn about the mutual understanding that can emerge from these interactions.
- **The Value of Listening:** Understand the importance of active listening during conversations with homeless individuals. Discover how validating their experiences and feelings can provide a sense of dignity.

Section 5.4.4: The Ripple Effect of Kindness

Acts of Kindness Challenge

Consider taking on an "Acts of Kindness Challenge" as a way to incorporate compassion into your daily life. We provide a list of actionable ideas to get you started:

- **Creating Positive Ripples:** Understand how small acts of kindness can create a ripple effect within communities. Witness the impact that acts of compassion have on both individuals and society as a whole.
- **The Ongoing Journey:** Recognize that kindness is not a one-time event but an ongoing journey. Explore how acts of kindness can become a way of life, enriching your own experience and the lives of those you touch.

Conclusion: The Ripple Effect of Compassion

As we conclude this section, we are reminded that compassion is not just an emotion; it's a driving force for change, and it can lead to transformative action. The stories of individuals and communities that have extended acts of kindness serve as beacons of hope, demonstrating the potential for change.

Chapter 6: 30 Days Without a Roof

Introduction to the Homelessness Challenge

In this chapter, we delve into the heart of the Homelessness Challenge—a transformative experience designed to immerse you in the reality of homelessness. Over the next 30 days, you will walk in the shoes of those who face the harsh realities of life without a roof over their heads. Through this journey, you will gain a deeper understanding of the challenges, survival strategies, and profound insights that emerge when your home is the streets.

Section 6.1: The First Night on the Streets

Embracing Uncertainty

As the sun sets on the first night of the challenge, you confront the uncertainty of life without shelter. We explore the emotions and practical challenges that arise during those initial hours of vulnerability:

- **The Weight of Darkness:** Experience the disorientation that accompanies the onset of darkness. The search for a safe and inconspicuous spot to rest becomes paramount.
- **Weathering the Elements:** Confront the harsh realities of exposure to the elements. Learn about the significance of warmth, protection, and improvised shelter.

Section 6.2: Survival Strategies and Realities

Navigating the Unpredictable

With each passing day, you adapt to the demands of street life. This section guides you through the survival strategies that homeless individuals employ:

- **Finding Food:** Explore the various methods of sourcing sustenance, from food banks and soup kitchens to scavenging and panhandling. The daily quest for nourishment becomes a fundamental task.
- **Staying Safe:** Understand the vigilance required to protect yourself and your few belongings on the streets. Learn about the risks and challenges posed by theft, violence, and the unpredictability of life.

Section 6.3: Reflections and Insights

The Depths of Solitude

As the days progress, moments of solitude offer opportunities for reflection. We delve into the profound insights that emerge during this journey:

- **The Isolation of Homelessness:** Experience the emotional toll of isolation and the yearning for connection. Understand how social disconnection can affect mental and emotional well-being.
- **Gratitude and Perspective:** Gain a newfound appreciation for the comforts and security of a stable home. Reflect on the role of gratitude in fostering resilience and empathy.

Section 6.4: The Final Days and Lessons

Completing the Challenge

As you approach the end of the 30-day challenge, you face a unique blend of emotions and lessons. This section offers guidance on completing the experience and transitioning back to stable housing:

- **The Final Stretch:** Navigate the final days with a mix of relief and nostalgia. Reflect on the lessons learned and the transformations that have taken place.
- **Carrying Forward Insights:** Explore how the insights gained from the challenge can influence your perspective on homelessness, advocacy, and community engagement. Consider the role you can play in making a difference.

Conclusion: A Deeper Understanding

As we conclude this chapter, you have embarked on a transformative journey into the world of homelessness. Through the Homelessness Challenge, you have gained firsthand insights into the challenges, survival strategies, and emotional landscapes of those living on the streets.

Section 6.1: The First Night on the Streets

Embracing Uncertainty

The first night of the Homelessness Challenge is upon you. As the sun sets and the city transforms, you find yourself at the precipice of an experience that will change your perspective forever. This section will guide you through the emotions, challenges, and essential survival strategies you encounter during those initial hours of vulnerability.

The Weight of Darkness

The transition from the familiar comforts of a home to the harsh realities of the streets can be overwhelming. In the quiet of night, you face the weight of darkness:

- **The Disorientation:** Explore the sense of disorientation that accompanies the onset of darkness. The bustling streets you once knew take on a different character as they become your temporary home.
- **The Search for Shelter:** Understand the urgency of finding a safe and inconspicuous spot to rest. The quest for shelter, even if it's a secluded corner or a hidden alcove, becomes a priority.
- **Facing Uncertainty:** Confront the uncertainty that lingers in the air. You have no permanent roof over your head, and this newfound reality brings both fear and an opportunity for introspection.

Weathering the Elements

As the night progresses, you become acutely aware of your exposure to the elements. Weather conditions can be unforgiving, and the need for warmth and protection becomes paramount:

- **The Chill in the Air:** Experience the biting cold that seeps into your bones. Learn about the importance of layered clothing and improvised insulation to ward off the cold.
- **Rain and Unpredictability:** Contend with rain as it threatens to soak your meager belongings. Understand the vulnerability of your makeshift shelter and the unpredictability of weather patterns.
- **Making Do with Limited Resources:** Discover how resourcefulness comes into play as you make do with limited supplies. From using discarded cardboard for insulation to seeking refuge in public spaces, every decision becomes a calculated move for survival.

Community and Camaraderie

While the streets may seem lonely, you'll begin to notice the presence of others who share this journey. Some may be fellow participants in the challenge, while others are individuals experiencing homelessness. The sense of camaraderie among those facing similar circumstances provides a glimmer of connection:

- **Shared Experiences:** Connect with others who understand the challenges you face. Share stories, offer assistance when needed, and recognize the strength that emerges from unity.

- **The Importance of Safety:** Understand the significance of safety in numbers. Learn about the informal networks that exist among individuals experiencing homelessness, where collective watchfulness provides a layer of security.
- **The Human Connection:** Embrace the moments of genuine human connection that can occur on the streets. Sometimes, a brief conversation or a shared meal can offer solace and a sense of belonging.

Conclusion: The First Steps Into the Unknown

As you conclude your first night on the streets, you have taken your first steps into the unknown. The darkness and uncertainty that enveloped you have begun to reveal the realities of life without a roof over your head.

Section 6.2: Survival Strategies and Realities

Navigating the Unpredictable

As the days pass in the Homelessness Challenge, you begin to adapt to the demands of street life. This section explores the essential survival strategies that homeless individuals employ daily to meet their basic needs and confront the harsh realities of life without stable housing.

Finding Food

One of the most immediate and critical concerns when experiencing homelessness is finding food. This section delves into the various methods and challenges of sourcing sustenance:

- **The Quest for Sustenance:** Explore the daily quest for food that becomes a fundamental task. Learn about the reliance on food banks, soup kitchens, and charitable organizations to meet nutritional needs.
- **Scavenging and Panhandling:** Understand the resourcefulness required to source food from unconventional places. Explore the practice of panhandling and the stigma that often accompanies it.
- **The Role of Community:** Recognize the importance of community and mutual support in sharing meals and resources. Discover how homeless individuals come together to help one another.

Staying Safe

Navigating the streets while homeless presents numerous safety challenges. This section delves into the vigilance required to protect yourself and your few belongings:

- **The Vulnerability of Possessions:** Understand the constant threat of theft and the need to safeguard your meager possessions. Learn about strategies to keep belongings secure.
- **Violence and Conflict:** Explore the risk of violence and conflicts that can arise within the homeless community or from external sources. Understand the dynamics of safety concerns and the need to stay vigilant.
- **The Unpredictability of Life:** Confront the unpredictable nature of life on the streets. From encounters with law enforcement to unexpected weather changes, learn how to adapt and respond to unforeseen challenges.

Building Resilience

Surviving homelessness requires not only practical skills but also resilience in the face of adversity. This section explores the emotional and psychological aspects of homelessness:

- **Emotional Toll:** Understand the emotional toll of homelessness, including feelings of isolation, loneliness, and the strain of living in a constant state of vulnerability.
- **Coping Mechanisms:** Explore the coping mechanisms that homeless individuals develop to deal with stress and uncertainty. From peer support to self-soothing techniques, resilience takes many forms.
- **The Strength of the Human Spirit:** Recognize the strength and resilience of homeless individuals who face daily challenges with determination and courage. Learn how their experiences can inspire and inform your own journey.

Conclusion: Navigating the Unseen Realities

As you navigate the unpredictable realities of life without stable housing, you gain insights into the resilience and resourcefulness required to survive on the streets. The challenges you face mirror those encountered by countless individuals experiencing homelessness every day.

Section 6.3: Reflections and Insights

The Depths of Solitude

As the days progress in the Homelessness Challenge, moments of solitude become increasingly prevalent. During these solitary moments, you have the opportunity for deep reflection, introspection, and the emergence of profound insights into the human condition.

The Isolation of Homelessness

One of the most striking aspects of homelessness is the isolation it can bring. This section explores the emotional toll of isolation and the yearning for connection:

- **The Loneliness:** Experience the profound sense of loneliness that often accompanies homelessness. Understand how it feels to be disconnected from the routines and social interactions that define everyday life.
- **Yearning for Connection:** Explore the deep yearning for connection and human contact. Discover how the absence of these fundamental aspects of life can affect your emotional well-being.
- **The Role of Self-Reliance:** Understand the need for self-reliance in the absence of a stable support system. Learn about the strategies that homeless individuals develop to rely on themselves in moments of solitude.

Gratitude and Perspective

As you grapple with the isolation of homelessness, you begin to appreciate the simple comforts and securities that stable housing provides. This section delves into the role of gratitude and perspective:

- **Finding Gratitude:** Explore how moments of solitude can lead to the cultivation of gratitude. Learn how homeless individuals find reasons to be thankful, even in the midst of adversity.
- **Perspective Shifts:** Understand the transformative power of perspective shifts. Witness how the challenges and hardships of homelessness can lead to a deeper understanding of the value of stability and security.
- **Empathy and Understanding:** Recognize the potential for greater empathy and understanding as you reflect on your experiences. Consider how these insights can inform your interactions with homeless individuals and your advocacy efforts.

The Inner Journey

In moments of solitude and introspection, you embark on an inner journey that transcends the physical realities of homelessness. This section explores the inner landscape that unfolds during your journey:

- **Self-Discovery:** Delve into the process of self-discovery that occurs as you confront your own vulnerabilities and limitations. Understand how these discoveries can shape your identity and values.
- **The Power of Resilience:** Reflect on the resilience that emerges from the depths of solitude. Learn how the challenges you face foster inner strength and fortitude.
- **The Intersection of Humanity:** Recognize the shared experiences and common humanity that connect you with homeless individuals. Explore how these connections can lead to greater empathy and compassion.

Conclusion: Illuminating the Inner Self

As you conclude this section, you have embarked on an inner journey that mirrors the external challenges of homelessness. The solitude, reflection, and insights gained during this time provide a unique perspective on the human experience.

Section 6.4: The Final Days and Lessons

Completing the Challenge

As the 30-day Homelessness Challenge nears its conclusion, you find yourself at the intersection of an extraordinary experience and a transformative journey. This section guides you through the final days of the challenge, the mix of emotions you encounter, and the valuable lessons that will stay with you as you move forward.

The Final Stretch

In the waning days of the challenge, a mix of emotions—relief, nostalgia, and introspection—permeates your experience. This section explores the significance of the final stretch:

- **The Relief of Transition:** Experience a sense of relief as the end of the challenge approaches. Understand the comfort and security that await you, and reflect on what these mean to you now.
- **Nostalgia for the Streets:** Confront the nostalgia for the streets and the unique connections you've forged during the challenge. Explore the complex emotions that arise as you prepare to leave this temporary reality.

- **The Weight of Reflection:** Reflect on the lessons learned and the transformations you've undergone. Consider how your perspective on homelessness and empathy for those experiencing it have evolved.

Carrying Forward Insights

As you prepare to leave behind the challenges of the streets, you carry forward a wealth of insights and experiences. This section examines how these insights can influence your perspective on homelessness and your role in creating positive change:

- **The Ripple Effect of Compassion:** Understand the potential for your newfound insights to create a ripple effect of compassion. Explore how your journey can inspire those around you to take action.
- **Advocacy and Community Engagement:** Reflect on the ways in which you can channel your experiences into advocacy and community engagement. Consider the role you can play in raising awareness and advocating for solutions.
- **The Power of Personal Transformation:** Recognize the personal transformation that has taken place over the course of the challenge. Explore how these changes can enrich your own life and the lives of others.

A Deeper Understanding

As you conclude the Homelessness Challenge, you have gained a deeper understanding of the challenges, survival strategies, and emotional landscapes of those experiencing homelessness. Your journey has mirrored their world, allowing you to approach the issue with newfound empathy and insight.

Chapter 7: Stepping into the Shadows

Experiencing Homelessness Firsthand

In this chapter, you embark on a unique and powerful journey—stepping directly into the shadows of homelessness. It's a raw and unfiltered experience, one that will challenge your perceptions, expose you to unexpected encounters, take you on an emotional rollercoaster, and ultimately offer profound lessons about the human spirit and the realities of life on the streets.

Section 7.1: Challenges and Unexpected Encounters

Navigating the Unpredictable Terrain

As you immerse yourself in the world of homelessness, every day brings a new set of challenges and unforeseen encounters. This section explores the rollercoaster of emotions and experiences you encounter:

- **The Element of Surprise:** Embrace the unpredictability of life on the streets. Understand how every day is marked by uncertainty and adaptability.
- **Human Stories:** Encounter the diverse stories of individuals you meet along the way. From fellow challenge participants to those experiencing homelessness, each person's narrative adds depth to your understanding.
- **Moments of Vulnerability:** Confront moments of vulnerability, from encounters with law enforcement to navigating the intricacies of homeless encampments. Reflect on the emotional weight of these experiences.

Section 7.2: The Emotional Rollercoaster

Riding the Waves of Emotion

Life on the streets is an emotional rollercoaster. In this section, we explore the wide range of emotions you'll encounter and how they shape your perspective:

- **The Depths of Despair:** Experience moments of despair and hopelessness. Understand the emotional toll of uncertainty and the longing for stability.
- **Finding Joy and Connection:** Embrace moments of joy, camaraderie, and connection that can emerge even in the midst of adversity. Learn how human connection provides solace.
- **The Empathy Paradox:** Confront the paradox of empathy—the ability to feel deeply for others while experiencing your own hardships. Reflect on the power of empathy to motivate change.

Section 7.3: The Final Days and Lessons

Completing the Journey

As your journey into homelessness reaches its conclusion, this section guides you through the final days, the mix of emotions you encounter, and the profound lessons that will stay with you:

- **The Relief of Transition:** Experience a sense of relief as you prepare to leave behind the challenges of the streets. Reflect on the comfort and security that await you.
- **Nostalgia and Reflection:** Confront the nostalgia for the streets and the unique connections you've forged. Reflect on how these experiences have reshaped your understanding of homelessness.
- **The Lessons Learned:** Reflect on the invaluable lessons you've learned throughout this journey. Consider how your perspective on homelessness and your capacity for empathy have evolved.

Conclusion: Emerging from the Shadows

As you conclude this chapter and your immersion into homelessness, you emerge from the shadows with a profound understanding of the complexities of life on the streets. Your experiences have illuminated the human spirit, the power of empathy, and the urgent need for change.

Section 7.1: Challenges and Unexpected Encounters

Navigating the Unpredictable Terrain

As you step into the shadows of homelessness, each day presents a new set of challenges, encounters, and emotions. The unpredictable nature of life on the streets becomes a central theme, and in this section, we delve into the rollercoaster of experiences you'll face during your immersion.

The Element of Surprise

Life on the streets is marked by unpredictability. Every day brings new challenges, encounters, and uncertainties that test your adaptability and resilience:

- **Dawn of the Unknown:** Embrace the uncertainty of each day. Explore the unpredictability of your environment as you navigate the streets, knowing that each corner turned could reveal a new challenge or opportunity.
- **Adapt or Perish:** Understand the necessity of adaptability. Discover how homeless individuals develop an acute sense of adaptability, learning to respond quickly and effectively to changing circumstances.
- **The Unseen Challenges:** Confront the challenges that are invisible to those with stable housing. From finding a place to sleep to securing your belongings, each day poses unique hurdles that require creative solutions.

Human Stories

As you journey through homelessness, you'll encounter a diverse array of individuals, each with their own story to tell. These stories add depth to your understanding of the homeless experience:

- **Fellow Participants:** Meet fellow participants in the challenge, each with their own motivations and backgrounds. Share your experiences and learn from one another's perspectives.
- **Those Experiencing Homelessness:** Engage with individuals who are living on the streets as a way of life. Listen to their stories, challenges, and aspirations. Gain insights into the resilience and resourcefulness that define their daily lives.
- **The Complexity of Compassion:** Explore the complexities of offering help and compassion. Understand the balance between respecting the autonomy of homeless individuals and providing support when it's needed most.

Moments of Vulnerability

During your immersion into homelessness, moments of vulnerability will be frequent. From interactions with law enforcement to navigating the dynamics of homeless encampments, you'll experience a wide range of emotions:

- **Encounters with Law Enforcement:** Navigate encounters with law enforcement, which can range from routine interactions to more challenging situations. Reflect on the emotional weight of these encounters and the impact on your sense of safety.
- **Navigating Homeless Communities:** Gain insight into the intricacies of homeless encampments and communities. Learn about the unwritten rules, hierarchies, and dynamics that define these spaces.
- **The Emotional Toll:** Confront the emotional toll of homelessness. From frustration to fear and compassion to camaraderie, the emotional landscape of the streets is complex and ever-shifting.

Conclusion: Navigating the Unseen Realities

As you conclude this section, you have navigated the unpredictable terrain of homelessness, gaining firsthand experience of the challenges, encounters, and emotions that define life on the streets. Your journey mirrors the daily realities of countless individuals facing homelessness, and it offers a window into the complexities of their world.

Section 7.2: The Emotional Rollercoaster

Riding the Waves of Emotion

As you journey through homelessness, you'll find that life on the streets is a profound emotional rollercoaster. This section explores the myriad emotions you'll experience during your immersion, how they impact your perspective, and the ways in which they shape your understanding of homelessness.

The Depths of Despair

Homelessness can often bring moments of deep despair and hopelessness. In this section, you'll delve into the emotional toll of uncertainty and the longing for stability:

- **The Weight of Uncertainty:** Experience the emotional weight of uncertainty that accompanies homelessness. Understand how not knowing where you'll sleep or how you'll find your next meal can take a toll on your well-being.
- **Longing for Stability:** Confront the longing for stability and security. Explore the profound desire for a place to call home and the sense of stability that it represents.
- **The Strain of Survival:** Recognize the mental and emotional strain of living in a constant state of vulnerability. Understand how the pressures of survival can contribute to feelings of despair.

Finding Joy and Connection

Despite the challenges of homelessness, moments of joy, camaraderie, and connection can emerge even in the midst of adversity. This section explores the resilience of the human spirit:

- **Moments of Joy:** Embrace moments of joy that can be found even in unexpected places. Discover how simple pleasures, such as a shared meal or a kind gesture, can brighten your day.
- **Camaraderie Among Peers:** Recognize the sense of camaraderie that exists among individuals experiencing homelessness. Learn how shared experiences create bonds and support networks.
- **The Power of Human Connection:** Reflect on the power of human connection in moments of vulnerability. Understand how reaching out to others and offering kindness can provide solace and hope.

The Empathy Paradox

As you navigate the emotional rollercoaster of homelessness, you'll confront the paradox of empathy—the ability to feel deeply for others while experiencing your own hardships:

- **Balancing Empathy:** Explore the challenges of balancing your empathy for others with your own struggles. Consider the emotional toll of bearing witness to the suffering of fellow homeless individuals.
- **Motivating Change:** Reflect on how empathy can be a powerful motivator for change. Understand how the empathy you feel can drive you to advocate for solutions to homelessness and work toward a more compassionate society.
- **The Resilience of Empathy:** Recognize the resilience of empathy and its capacity to endure even in the face of adversity. Consider how your empathy evolves and deepens throughout your journey.

Section 7.3: The Final Days and Lessons

Completing the Journey

As your journey through homelessness approaches its conclusion, a mix of emotions—relief, nostalgia, and introspection—permeates your experience. This section guides you through the final days, the emotional landscape you encounter, and the profound lessons that will stay with you as you move forward.

The Relief of Transition

In the waning days of your immersion into homelessness, a sense of relief washes over you. This section explores the significance of this transition:

- **Anticipation of Change:** Experience the anticipation of returning to the comforts of stable housing. Reflect on how the prospect of a warm bed and a hot meal impacts your outlook.
- **Comfort and Security:** Confront the stark contrast between life on the streets and the security of a stable home. Reflect on how this newfound comfort affects your perspective.
- **The Complexity of Relief:** Understand the complexity of relief, which is tinged with gratitude, guilt, and the recognition of privilege. Explore the emotional nuances of leaving behind the challenges of homelessness.

Nostalgia and Reflection

As your journey comes to an end, nostalgia for the streets and the unique connections you've forged becomes palpable. This section delves into the complex emotions you experience:

- **The Pull of Nostalgia:** Confront the nostalgia for the streets and the sense of camaraderie you've built with fellow participants and individuals experiencing homelessness.
- **Emotional Attachments:** Reflect on the emotional attachments you've formed during your journey. Consider the bonds you've forged with those who shared this unique experience.
- **Reshaping Your Understanding:** Understand how these experiences have reshaped your understanding of homelessness. Explore the emotional landscape of empathy and compassion.

The Lessons Learned

As you prepare to leave behind the challenges of the streets, you carry forward a wealth of insights and experiences. This section examines how these lessons can influence your perspective on homelessness and your role in creating positive change:

- **The Ripple Effect of Compassion:** Reflect on how your newfound insights have the potential to create a ripple effect of compassion. Explore how your journey can inspire those around you to take action.
- **Advocacy and Community Engagement:** Consider the ways in which you can channel your experiences into advocacy and community engagement. Reflect on the role you can play in raising awareness and advocating for solutions.
- **The Power of Personal Transformation:** Recognize the personal transformation that has taken place over the course of your journey. Understand how these changes can enrich your own life and the lives of others.

Section 7.4: A Deeper Understanding

Transcending the Surface

As you conclude your immersive journey into homelessness, you emerge with a profound understanding of the complexities, nuances, and layers that define life on the streets. This section explores how your experiences have deepened your comprehension of homelessness, the shared humanity that connects us all, and the potential for positive change.

Unveiling Complexity

Your journey has unveiled the intricate web of challenges, emotions, and survival strategies that homeless individuals navigate daily. In this section, we delve into the depth of this complexity:

- **The Multifaceted Homelessness Experience:** Reflect on the multifaceted nature of homelessness, encompassing a wide range of experiences, backgrounds, and circumstances. Understand that there is no one-size-fits-all narrative.
- **The Intersection of Vulnerabilities:** Recognize how homelessness often intersects with other vulnerabilities, such as mental health issues, addiction, and trauma. Consider the additional challenges that individuals facing these intersecting vulnerabilities encounter.
- **The Role of Systemic Factors:** Explore how systemic factors, including housing affordability, social services, and economic disparities, contribute to the homelessness crisis. Understand that addressing homelessness requires systemic change.

Shared Humanity

Through your immersion, you've encountered the shared humanity that connects all individuals, regardless of their housing status. This section explores the ways in which you've discovered this shared humanity:

- **Breaking Down Stereotypes:** Reflect on how your experiences have shattered stereotypes and preconceived notions about homelessness. Understand that homelessness does not define an individual's worth or character.
- **Empathy and Connection:** Recognize the power of empathy and connection in bridging the gap between individuals with and without stable housing. Consider how these connections have enriched your perspective.
- **Collective Responsibility:** Understand that homelessness is not an isolated issue affecting only a few. It is a societal challenge that calls for collective responsibility and a commitment to finding solutions that benefit all.

The Potential for Positive Change

Your immersion into homelessness has left an indelible mark on your understanding of the issue. In this section, we explore the potential for positive change:

- **Advocacy and Awareness:** Reflect on your role as an advocate for change. Consider how your experiences can be a catalyst for raising awareness and advocating for policies and initiatives that address homelessness.

- **Community Engagement:** Explore opportunities for community engagement and collaboration. Understand that meaningful change often arises from partnerships between individuals, organizations, and government agencies.
- **The Power of Personal Transformation:** Recognize how your journey has transformed not only your perspective on homelessness but also your own life. Consider how your newfound empathy and insights can inspire others to act.

Conclusion: Illuminating the Path Forward

As you conclude this section and your immersive journey, you've gained a deeper understanding of the complexity of homelessness, the shared humanity that binds us all, and the potential for positive change. Armed with empathy, insights, and a commitment to making a difference, you are prepared to continue your exploration "Beyond the Streets."

I

Act 1: The Homelessness Challenge - Could You?

Summary and Conclusion

In Act 1 of our journey, we embarked on a profound exploration of homelessness. We challenged ourselves and our readers to confront a fundamental question: Could you live without a home? This act has been a transformative and eye-opening experience, allowing us to gain firsthand insights into the challenges and realities of homelessness. As we conclude this act, we reflect on the seven chapters that have taken us through the emotional and impactful journey of experiencing homelessness.

Chapter 1: The Homelessness Challenge

Summary

Chapter 1 set the stage for our journey, introducing the concept of the Homelessness Challenge—a 30-day immersion into homelessness. We explored the motivations behind this unique experience, acknowledging the growing crisis of homelessness and our commitment to understanding it on a deeper level. The chapter provided an overview of what lay ahead, challenging readers to question their assumptions and biases about homelessness.

Conclusion

As we conclude Chapter 1, we recognize the importance of empathy and understanding in addressing homelessness. The Homelessness Challenge is not only a personal exploration but also a call to action. By undertaking this challenge, we have already taken the first step toward making a difference.

Chapter 2: Homelessness Unveiled

Summary

Chapter 2, titled "Homelessness Unveiled," was a deep dive into the multifaceted world of homelessness. We began by sharing stories from the streets, shedding light on the diverse experiences and backgrounds of those experiencing homelessness. The chapter then explored the daily struggles faced by homeless individuals, from finding food and shelter to coping with the emotional toll of uncertainty. We examined the fundamental need for safety and shelter and the harsh realities of life on the streets. Additionally, we delved into the role of stigma and stereotypes in perpetuating misconceptions about homelessness.

Conclusion

In the conclusion of Chapter 2, we reflect on the power of storytelling to break down stereotypes and build empathy. By sharing the stories of individuals experiencing homelessness, we've humanized a crisis that often remains hidden in the shadows. As we move forward, we carry with us a deeper understanding of the challenges faced by our fellow community members.

Chapter 3: Beyond the Streets

Summary

Chapter 3, titled "Beyond the Streets," shifted our focus from understanding homelessness to exploring solutions and approaches. We delved into the concept of Housing First initiatives, which prioritize stable housing as the first step toward addressing homelessness. Supportive services and programs designed to help homeless individuals on their path to recovery and stability were also examined. The chapter emphasized the importance of advocacy and policy change in creating systemic solutions to homelessness.

Conclusion

In the conclusion of Chapter 3, we recognize that homelessness is not an insurmountable problem but a challenge that can be addressed through thoughtful policies and collaborative efforts. Housing First initiatives and supportive services offer tangible paths to recovery and stability for homeless individuals. Our journey has revealed that positive change is possible when we advocate for systemic solutions.

Chapter 4: From Shelter to Hope

Summary

Chapter 4, titled "From Shelter to Hope," guided readers through the process of preparing for the Homelessness Challenge. We explored the practical aspects of navigating life on the margins, from securing essential items to understanding the importance of community support. The chapter also emphasized the role of empathy and compassion in shaping our mindset as we prepared for the challenge.

Conclusion

In the conclusion of Chapter 4, we recognize that preparation for the Homelessness Challenge extends beyond gathering physical resources; it involves cultivating a mindset of empathy and compassion. Our journey has taught us that these qualities are essential for understanding and connecting with those experiencing homelessness.

Chapter 5: Faces of Resilience

Summary

Chapter 5, "Faces of Resilience," shifted our focus to the individuals who have faced homelessness and emerged as resilient survivors. We shared success stories that highlighted the strength and determination of homeless individuals who have overcome adversity. The chapter emphasized the role of community support and solidarity in empowering those experiencing homelessness and the valuable lessons we can learn from their experiences.

Conclusion

In the conclusion of Chapter 5, we celebrate the resilience of individuals who have faced homelessness and emerged stronger. Their stories serve as a source of inspiration and hope, reminding us that even in the face of daunting challenges, the human spirit has the capacity to persevere.

Chapter 6: 30 Days Without a Roof

Summary

Chapter 6 marked the beginning of the Homelessness Challenge itself. Titled "30 Days Without a Roof," this chapter took readers through the first days of our journey on the streets. We experienced the challenges of the first night without shelter, explored survival strategies, and embarked on a reflective journey that allowed us to gain insights into the harsh realities of homelessness.

Conclusion

In the conclusion of Chapter 6, we acknowledge the emotional and physical challenges of our first days on the streets. We recognize that the Homelessness Challenge is not just an experiment but an opportunity to gain deep insights into the struggles faced by homeless individuals. As we navigate this experience, we embrace the need for reflection and self-discovery.

Chapter 7: Stepping into the Shadows

Summary

Chapter 7, "Stepping into the Shadows," deepened our immersion into homelessness. We explored the challenges and unexpected encounters that arose during our journey. From interactions with law enforcement to navigating homeless communities, we confronted the emotional rollercoaster of our experiences on the streets. The chapter also highlighted the importance of maintaining empathy and compassion in the face of adversity.

Conclusion

In the conclusion of Chapter 7, we recognize that the challenges and encounters of homelessness are unpredictable and emotionally charged. We have learned to navigate the unknown with resilience and to embrace the complexities of empathy and compassion. Our journey has illuminated the importance of maintaining a compassionate mindset even in the face of adversity.

Conclusion to Act 1: A Journey of Understanding and Empathy

As we conclude Act 1 of our journey, we reflect on the transformative experiences and insights gained. We have ventured into the shadows of homelessness, experiencing the emotional highs and lows, confronting stereotypes, and understanding the challenges faced by those living on the streets. Our journey has been a testament to the power of empathy, compassion, and human connection.

In Act 2, we will shift our focus to "Making a Difference." Armed with a deeper understanding of homelessness and a commitment to change, we will explore solutions, advocacy efforts, and the potential for positive impact. Our journey continues, and the opportunity to make a difference lies ahead.

In the words of Mahatma Gandhi, "You must be the change you want to see in the world." Act 1 has been a journey of self-discovery and understanding. Act 2 will be a journey of action and advocacy. Together, we will strive to create a more compassionate society, where homelessness is not just a challenge endured in the shadows but a problem addressed with empathy, compassion, and effective solutions.

ACT 2

INTRODUCTION

Act 2: Making a Difference

Introduction

In Act 1 of our journey through the complexities of homelessness, we dared to ask a fundamental question: "Could you live without a home?" We ventured into the shadows, experiencing firsthand the challenges, emotions, and resilience of individuals facing homelessness. We confronted stereotypes, immersed ourselves in the homeless community, and emerged with a deeper understanding of this pervasive issue.

As we step into Act 2, titled "Making a Difference," the focus shifts from personal exploration to collective action. We transition from the question of "Could you?" to the more profound query of "Would you make a difference?" Act 2 is a call to arms, a journey of advocacy, empathy, and commitment to change.

Chapter 8: Surviving the Streets

Reintegrating into Housed Life

Our journey continues by reflecting on the lives of those who have survived the streets. Reintegrating into housed life is not a simple process. The challenges that follow homelessness can be as daunting as the experience itself. The journey from street to shelter can be long and fraught with obstacles.

We delve into the stories of survivors who have navigated this path. They teach us that finding stable housing is just the beginning. Overcoming post-homelessness challenges, such as mental health recovery, substance abuse rehabilitation, and reconnecting with support networks, requires resilience and community support.

Coping with Post-Homelessness Challenges

Mental health recovery is a significant aspect of post-homelessness life. Many who have experienced homelessness grapple with trauma, depression, anxiety, and other mental health issues. Exiting homelessness involves accessing mental health support services, coping with past traumas, and rebuilding emotional well-being.

Substance abuse can be both a cause and a consequence of homelessness. Survivors must navigate the path to sobriety while managing the stressors of housed life. Substance abuse recovery often requires a multifaceted approach, including counseling, support groups, and treatment programs.

Reconnecting with support networks is vital for stability. Homelessness can strain family and social connections. Rebuilding these networks is a crucial step in regaining a sense of belonging and support.

The Long-Term Effects of the Experience

Homelessness leaves lasting imprints on those who have endured it. Trauma and resilience often coexist, shaping survivors' outlook on life. We explore how these experiences can influence their emotional well-being and coping mechanisms.

Economic instability is another challenge that persists. Exiting homelessness often means facing financial hurdles. The struggle to find stable employment and housing can be ongoing, affecting survivors' financial security.

Advocacy and activism frequently emerge as survivors seek to address systemic issues. Many become advocates for the homeless community, leveraging their experiences to drive change. We share stories of individuals who have turned their struggles into a powerful force for good.

Advocacy and Activism

Advocacy and activism are potent tools in the fight against homelessness. In this section, we explore their critical role in creating lasting change. Advocates and activists raise awareness, drive policy change, and support organizations that provide essential services to homeless individuals.

Raising awareness begins with dispelling myths and stereotypes. Advocates use their voices to educate communities about the realities of homelessness, humanizing those affected by it.

Policy change is essential for addressing the systemic factors contributing to homelessness. We examine the impact of policies on homelessness and how advocates work tirelessly to reform them. Policy advocacy involves collaborating with policymakers, conducting research, and mobilizing grassroots efforts.

Supporting organizations that provide essential services to homeless individuals is another avenue for making a difference. Advocates often partner with shelters, food banks, and mental health organizations to extend help to those in need.

Conclusion: A Journey of Survival, Recovery, and Advocacy

Chapter 8 emphasizes the resilience of those who have survived the streets. It underscores the challenges they face in reintegrating into housed life and the importance of advocacy and activism in shaping a better future.

As we move forward in Act 2, let us remember the stories of survivors and draw inspiration from their journeys of survival, recovery, and advocacy. Act 2 is a call to action—a call to explore root causes, systemic issues, and the power of empathy. It's a call to reflect on the impact of our Homelessness Challenge and the role each of us can play in making a difference.

In Act 2, we'll delve deeper into the underlying causes of homelessness, the complexities of mental health, addiction, and poverty, and the ways in which individuals, communities, and organizations are working tirelessly to effect change. Our journey continues, and the potential for making a difference is within our grasp.

Together, let us embrace Act 2 as we explore "Making a Difference."

Chapter 8: Surviving the Streets

Reintegrating into Housed Life

The journey from homelessness to stability is often seen as a triumphant leap from despair to hope. Yet, the reality is more complex. Exiting homelessness can be as challenging, if not more so, than enduring life on the streets. The transition from the harsh environment of homelessness to the comforts of a sheltered life is not a linear path. It is a journey marked by hurdles, setbacks, and the need for resilience and community support.

In this chapter, we explore the stories of those who have survived the streets and reintegrated into housed life. We delve into the post-homelessness challenges they face, the long-term effects of their experiences, and the role of advocacy and activism in their journeys.

Coping with Post-Homelessness Challenges

Homelessness leaves a profound impact on individuals, not only during their time on the streets but also as they attempt to rebuild their lives. As we shift our focus from life on the streets to the transition into housed life, we must acknowledge the multifaceted challenges faced by survivors.

- **Mental Health Recovery**

The harsh realities of homelessness often lead to mental health struggles. Trauma, isolation, and the constant threat to one's safety can leave lasting emotional scars. Reintegrating into housed life involves addressing these mental health challenges.

Jennifer's Story: Jennifer, a survivor of homelessness, shares her journey of mental health recovery. She discusses the importance of accessible mental health services and the ongoing process of healing.

- **Substance Abuse Recovery**

Substance abuse is a prevalent issue among homeless individuals, sometimes as a coping mechanism for the difficulties they face. For those who have struggled with addiction, finding stability involves navigating the path to sobriety.

James' Journey: James, a survivor who battled addiction while homeless, opens up about his recovery journey. He sheds light on the complexities of achieving sobriety and staying on that path post-homelessness.

- **Reconnecting with Support Networks**

Homelessness often strains relationships with family and friends. The process of reintegration includes rebuilding these essential support networks, which are crucial for emotional well-being and stability.

Sarah's Reunion: Sarah, a former homeless individual, shares her experience of reconnecting with her family after years of estrangement. Her story illustrates the challenges and rewards of mending fractured relationships.

The Long-Term Effects of the Experience

Homelessness leaves enduring imprints on those who have faced it. The transition into housed life may mark the end of a chapter, but it doesn't erase the experiences that came before. The long-term effects of homelessness can shape the trajectory of survivors' lives.

- **Trauma and Resilience**

Survivors often carry the weight of trauma with them. Their resilience is remarkable, but the scars remain. We explore how these experiences shape their outlook on life and the challenges they face in dealing with past traumas.

David's Resilience: David, a survivor who overcame homelessness, discusses how his experiences have influenced his approach to life. He reflects on the balance between trauma and resilience.

- **Economic Instability**

Exiting homelessness doesn't guarantee immediate economic stability. Finding stable employment and housing can be an ongoing struggle. Survivors may face financial hurdles as they attempt to regain their footing.

Rebecca's Financial Journey: Rebecca shares her experiences of securing stable employment and housing after homelessness. She emphasizes the financial obstacles she encountered and the importance of financial literacy.

- **Advocacy and Activism**

For many survivors, the journey from homelessness to stability leads to advocacy and activism. Their firsthand experiences propel them to become advocates for the homeless community, using their voices to bring about change.

- **Raising Awareness**

Advocacy begins with raising awareness about the realities of homelessness. Survivors use their voices to educate communities, dispelling myths and stereotypes. We explore how their personal stories can create powerful impact.

Sam's Awareness Campaign: Sam, a survivor turned advocate, describes his efforts to raise awareness about homelessness in his community. He discusses the impact of personal storytelling in changing perceptions.

- **Policy Change**

Advocacy extends beyond awareness to policy change. Survivors collaborate with policymakers, conduct research, and mobilize grassroots efforts to reform policies that perpetuate homelessness.

Maria's Policy Advocacy: Maria, a former homeless individual, shares her journey of advocating for policy changes to improve access to affordable housing. Her story underscores the power of grassroots activism in driving systemic change.

- **Supporting Organizations**

Advocates often form partnerships with organizations that provide essential services to homeless individuals. These collaborations amplify their impact and extend much-needed help to those in need.

Michael's Collaboration: Michael, an advocate, discusses his partnership with a local shelter and food bank to support homeless individuals. He highlights the importance of community partnerships in addressing homelessness.

Conclusion: A Journey of Survival, Recovery, and Advocacy

Chapter 8 has taken us on a journey through the lives of those who have survived the streets. We've explored their efforts to reintegrate into housed life, coping with post-homelessness challenges, and the long-term effects of their experiences. Additionally, we've witnessed the power of advocacy and activism as survivors become champions for change.

As we move forward in Act 2, let us remember the resilience of survivors and draw inspiration from their journeys of survival, recovery, and advocacy. Act 2 is a call to action—a call to explore root causes, systemic issues, and the power of empathy. It's a call to reflect on the impact of our Homelessness Challenge and the role each of us can play in making a difference.

8.1 Reintegrating into Housed Life

The journey from homelessness to housed life is often portrayed as a triumphant transition, a beacon of hope amid the shadows of despair. It's an image of individuals leaving behind the harsh realities of the streets for the comforts of a sheltered existence. However, the process of reintegrating into housed life is far from a straightforward path. It is a journey marked by complexities, challenges, and the need for resilience and community support.

In this section, we explore the intricacies of reintegrating into housed life. We recognize that securing stable housing is just the first step in a long road to recovery for those who have experienced homelessness. It's a journey that requires navigating various obstacles, both tangible and emotional.

The First Glimpse of Shelter

For those transitioning out of homelessness, the first taste of shelter is often a mix of relief and trepidation. The four walls of a room provide protection from the elements and a sense of security that the streets could never offer. Yet, it's also a stark reminder of the contrast between the past and the present.

James' Story: James, a survivor of homelessness, vividly recalls his first night in a shelter. "I couldn't believe I had a bed to myself," he says. "It was almost surreal. But it was also a night filled with anxiety about what lay ahead."

The Challenge of Stability

While a roof over one's head is a crucial milestone, it doesn't guarantee immediate stability. The transition from homelessness to housed life often comes with a new set of challenges. Financial concerns, securing employment, and adapting to the routines of housed life can be overwhelming.

Rebecca's Financial Journey: Rebecca, who successfully exited homelessness, recounts her experiences of securing stable employment and housing. "I thought finding a job and a place to live would be the end of my struggles," she says. "But it was just the beginning of a different kind of challenge."

The Emotional Rollercoaster

The emotional toll of homelessness doesn't vanish overnight. Survivors carry with them the memories of the streets, the traumas, and the resilience that got them through. Reintegrating into housed life often involves confronting these emotions and seeking support for the mental scars left behind.

David's Resilience: David, who emerged from homelessness, reflects on the emotional rollercoaster of the transition. "The memories never fade entirely," he shares. "But they become a part of your story, a reminder of the strength that got you here."

The Importance of Support Networks

The transition to housed life is not a solitary journey. Reconnecting with family and friends is a crucial step for emotional well-being and stability. However, this process can be fraught with challenges, as strained relationships must be mended.

Sarah's Reunion: Sarah's journey involved reuniting with her family after years of estrangement. "It was one of the most challenging but rewarding aspects of my transition," she says. "Rebuilding those connections was essential for my recovery."

Conclusion: The First Steps Towards Stability

Reintegrating into housed life is a significant achievement, but it's only the beginning of a survivor's journey. The road to stability is marked by financial hurdles, emotional challenges, and the importance of reconnecting with support networks. It's a process that requires resilience, patience, and the understanding that healing takes time.

8.2 Coping with Post-Homelessness Challenges

The journey from homelessness to housed life is not just about securing a roof overhead. It's a multifaceted transition marked by a series of challenges, especially when it comes to coping with the aftermath of homelessness. Survivors often face a myriad of post-homelessness challenges, including mental health recovery, substance abuse rehabilitation, and the re-establishment of fractured support networks. This section delves into the complexities of these challenges and the importance of addressing them as part of the journey to stability.

Mental Health Recovery

One of the most pervasive post-homelessness challenges is the toll it takes on mental health. The streets are a harsh and unforgiving environment, often leading to trauma, depression, anxiety, and other mental health issues. Reintegrating into housed life involves not only securing a place to live but also addressing the psychological scars left behind.

Jennifer's Story: Jennifer, a survivor of homelessness, opens up about her journey of mental health recovery. She describes the importance of accessible mental health services and the ongoing process of healing. "Homelessness left deep emotional wounds," she says. "But seeking help and having a support system made all the difference."

Substance Abuse Recovery

Substance abuse is both a cause and a consequence of homelessness. Many individuals turn to drugs or alcohol as a coping mechanism for the hardships of life on the streets. For those who have struggled with addiction, achieving and maintaining sobriety is a critical component of the journey toward stability.

James' Journey: James, a survivor who battled addiction while homeless, shares his experiences of recovery. He discusses the complexities of achieving sobriety and staying on that path post-homelessness. "Addiction is a formidable adversary," he says, "but it can be overcome with the right support."

Reconnecting with Support Networks

Homelessness can strain relationships with family and friends, leading to isolation and estrangement. Reconnecting with these vital support networks is crucial for emotional well-being and stability. However, the process of rebuilding fractured relationships can be a delicate and challenging endeavor.

Sarah's Reunion: Sarah's journey involved reuniting with her family after years of separation. She describes the difficulties and rewards of mending those relationships. "Rebuilding trust and connection takes time," she acknowledges, "but it's worth every effort."

The Journey Toward Emotional Healing

The emotional toll of homelessness doesn't disappear with the acquisition of stable housing. Survivors carry with them the memories, traumas, and resilience that helped them endure life on the streets. Emotional healing is an ongoing process that involves acknowledging and addressing these experiences.

David's Resilience: David, who emerged from homelessness, reflects on the emotional rollercoaster of his transition. "The memories never fully fade," he says, "but they become a part of your story—a testament to the strength that got you here."

Conclusion: A Journey of Healing

Coping with post-homelessness challenges is an integral part of the journey to stability. Mental health recovery, substance abuse rehabilitation, and reconnecting with support networks are essential components of emotional healing. Survivors illustrate that with determination, resilience, and the right support, it's possible to navigate these challenges and move toward a brighter future.

8.3 The Long-Term Effects of the Experience

The journey from homelessness to housed life represents a significant achievement, but it doesn't mark the end of one's relationship with the past. Homelessness leaves indelible imprints on those who have endured it. The transition into housed life may signal a new chapter, but it doesn't erase the experiences that came before. This section explores the long-term effects of homelessness and how survivors continue to shape their lives beyond the streets.

Trauma and Resilience

Homelessness is often a traumatic experience. Survivors endure harsh conditions, isolation, and threats to their safety. Yet, they also exhibit remarkable resilience in the face of adversity. The coexistence of trauma and resilience is a defining feature of the homelessness journey.

David's Resilience: David, who emerged from homelessness, reflects on the emotional toll of his experience. "The trauma never fully fades," he says, "but it becomes a part of your story—a testament to the strength that got you here."

Economic Instability

Exiting homelessness doesn't guarantee immediate economic stability. Survivors may continue to face financial hurdles as they attempt to regain their footing. Finding stable employment, securing housing, and managing finances can be ongoing challenges.

Rebecca's Financial Journey: Rebecca, who successfully exited homelessness, shares her experiences of navigating the financial aspects of her transition. She emphasizes the importance of financial literacy and planning for a stable future.

Advocacy and Activism

For many survivors, the journey from homelessness to stability leads to advocacy and activism. Their firsthand experiences propel them to become advocates for the homeless community, using their voices to bring about change.

Raising Awareness

Advocacy begins with raising awareness about the realities of homelessness. Survivors use their voices to educate communities, dispelling myths and stereotypes. Personal stories become powerful tools for changing perceptions.

Sam's Awareness Campaign: Sam, a survivor turned advocate, describes his efforts to raise awareness about homelessness in his community. He discusses the impact of personal storytelling in changing public perceptions.

Policy Change

Advocacy extends beyond awareness to policy change. Survivors collaborate with policymakers, conduct research, and mobilize grassroots efforts to reform policies that perpetuate homelessness. Policy advocacy is a powerful means of addressing the systemic factors contributing to homelessness.

Maria's Policy Advocacy: Maria, a former homeless individual, shares her journey of advocating for policy changes to improve access to affordable housing. Her story underscores the power of grassroots activism in driving systemic change.

Supporting Organizations

Advocates often form partnerships with organizations that provide essential services to homeless individuals. These collaborations amplify their impact and extend much-needed help to those in need. Supporting organizations is an avenue for making a tangible difference in the lives of the homeless community.

Michael's Collaboration: Michael, an advocate, discusses his partnership with a local shelter and food bank to support homeless individuals. He highlights the importance of community partnerships in addressing homelessness.

Conclusion: A Journey of Transformation

Chapter 8 has taken us on a journey through the lives of those who have survived the streets. We've explored their efforts to reintegrate into housed life, cope with post-homelessness challenges, and confront the long-term effects of their experiences. Additionally, we've witnessed the power of advocacy and activism as survivors become champions for change.

As we move forward in Act 2, let us remember the resilience of survivors and draw inspiration from their journeys of survival, recovery, and advocacy. Act 2 is a call to action—a call to explore root causes, systemic issues, and the power of empathy. It's a call to reflect on the impact of our Homelessness Challenge and the role each of us can play in making a difference.

8.4 Advocacy and Activism

For many survivors of homelessness, the journey from the streets to stability is not merely a personal triumph—it becomes a catalyst for broader change. Their firsthand experiences propel them into the realm of advocacy and activism, where they use their voices to raise awareness, drive policy reform, and support organizations that provide essential services to homeless individuals. In this section, we explore the transformative power of advocacy and activism in the lives of survivors and their impact on the fight against homelessness.

Raising Awareness

Advocacy often begins with the simple act of raising awareness about the realities of homelessness. Survivors become storytellers, sharing their personal journeys to educate communities, dispel myths, and humanize those affected by homelessness. These stories become a powerful force in changing public perceptions.

Sam's Awareness Campaign: Sam, a survivor turned advocate, describes his efforts to raise awareness about homelessness in his community. He conducts workshops, speaks at local events, and engages with schools to share his story. "Personal storytelling has a way of breaking down barriers and creating empathy," Sam notes.

Policy Change

Advocacy extends beyond awareness to the realm of policy change. Survivors, armed with firsthand knowledge of the challenges faced by homeless individuals, collaborate with policymakers, conduct research, and mobilize grassroots efforts to reform policies that perpetuate homelessness.

Maria's Policy Advocacy: Maria, a former homeless individual, shares her journey of advocating for policy changes aimed at improving access to affordable housing. She testifies at legislative hearings, works with advocacy groups, and engages in community organizing. "Policy advocacy is about making systemic change," Maria asserts.

Supporting Organizations

Advocates often forge partnerships with organizations that provide essential services to homeless individuals. These collaborations amplify their impact and extend much-needed help to those in need. By working hand in hand with shelters, food banks, mental health clinics, and addiction treatment centers, advocates make a tangible difference in the lives of the homeless community.

Michael's Collaboration: Michael, an advocate, discusses his partnership with a local shelter and food bank to support homeless individuals. He emphasizes the importance of community partnerships in addressing homelessness. "Our collaborative efforts strengthen the safety net for those in crisis," Michael says.

The Ripple Effect of Advocacy

Advocacy and activism have a ripple effect. Survivors who become advocates inspire others to join the cause. Communities become more engaged, and public sentiment shifts toward empathy and action. Advocates catalyze a chain reaction of change that extends beyond their individual efforts.

Sarah's Role as a Mentor: Sarah, who successfully emerged from homelessness, now mentors individuals facing similar challenges. Her journey from homelessness to stability, and later advocacy, serves as an inspiration to others. "When you see that change is possible, it becomes contagious," Sarah affirms.

Conclusion: Advocates for Change

Chapter 8 has taken us on a journey through the lives of those who have survived the streets. We've explored their efforts to reintegrate into housed life, cope with post-homelessness challenges, confront the long-term effects of their experiences, and embrace advocacy and activism as a means of creating lasting change.

Chapter 9: Beneath the Surface

Homelessness is a complex and multifaceted issue that extends far beyond the visible reality of individuals sleeping on the streets. To truly understand and address homelessness, we must delve beneath the surface, exploring the root causes and systemic issues that perpetuate this crisis. In this chapter, we embark on a journey to uncover these hidden dimensions, examining the interplay of factors such as mental health, addiction, poverty, inequality, and structural barriers.

Root Causes and Systemic Issues

The homelessness crisis is not a solitary problem but a manifestation of deeper-rooted societal issues. To effectively combat homelessness, we must acknowledge and address these root causes.

- **Poverty and Income Inequality**

Poverty is a central driving force behind homelessness. In a world with stark income disparities, many individuals and families find themselves unable to afford stable housing. We delve into the link between poverty, income inequality, and homelessness.

Ella's Struggle: Ella, a mother who faced homelessness, shares her experiences of trying to make ends meet while living on the edge of poverty. Her story highlights the precarious nature of financial stability.

- **Structural Barriers**

Structural barriers, including limited access to affordable housing, employment discrimination, and the criminalization of homelessness, compound the issue. We explore how these systemic challenges perpetuate homelessness.

Alex's Battle: Alex, an advocate for the homeless, discusses the structural barriers he encountered while trying to secure housing and employment after experiencing homelessness. He sheds light on the need for policy reforms.

Homelessness and Mental Health

Mental health issues are both a cause and consequence of homelessness. The lack of stable housing exacerbates existing mental health conditions, while untreated mental illnesses can contribute to homelessness.

- **The Vicious Cycle of Mental Health and Homelessness**

We examine the vicious cycle of mental health and homelessness, exploring how individuals can become trapped in a cycle of despair without proper support and access to treatment.

Emily's Struggle: Emily, who experienced homelessness while battling mental illness, shares her journey of seeking help. Her story underscores the importance of mental health services in preventing and addressing homelessness.

- **Breaking Down Stigmas**

Stigma surrounding mental health often prevents individuals from seeking the help they need. We explore initiatives aimed at reducing stigma and increasing access to mental health services.

Jack's Advocacy: Jack, an advocate for mental health awareness, discusses his efforts to destigmatize mental illness and promote mental health education. He emphasizes the role of community support in overcoming stigma.

Addiction and Substance Abuse

Addiction and substance abuse are prevalent issues among homeless individuals. We delve into the complex relationship between addiction and homelessness and the importance of harm reduction approaches.

- **A Path to Recovery**

Recovery from addiction is possible, even in the midst of homelessness. We hear stories of individuals who have overcome addiction and found hope on their journey to stability.

Olivia's Recovery: Olivia, a survivor who battled addiction while homeless, shares her experiences of recovery. Her story illustrates the challenges and rewards of achieving sobriety.

Conclusion: Unveiling the Complexity

Chapter 9 has peeled back the layers of homelessness, revealing the root causes and systemic issues that underlie this crisis. Poverty, income inequality, structural barriers, mental health, and addiction all play interconnected roles. To truly make a difference, we must confront these issues head-on and work collectively to effect lasting change.

9.1 Poverty and Income Inequality

In the heart of the homelessness crisis lies a stark and uncomfortable truth: poverty and income inequality are the driving forces behind many individuals and families finding themselves on the brink of homelessness. The gap between the haves and the have-nots continues to widen, leaving a growing number of people unable to secure stable housing. In this section, we delve into the intricate relationship between poverty, income inequality, and homelessness, shedding light on the factors that perpetuate this social issue.

The Faces of Poverty

Poverty wears many faces, and its manifestations are as diverse as the individuals it affects. To truly understand the issue, we must explore the multifaceted nature of poverty.

- **Ella's Struggle:** Ella's story offers a poignant glimpse into the life of a mother struggling to make ends meet on the edge of poverty. She describes the challenges of balancing work, childcare, and housing in the face of financial instability.

The Growing Gap

Income inequality is not a new phenomenon, but its magnitude has reached alarming proportions in recent years. We examine the widening gap between the wealthiest individuals and the rest of society and its implications for homelessness.

The Precarious Nature of Employment

The availability of stable employment plays a pivotal role in preventing homelessness. However, for many, securing steady work remains an elusive goal. We explore the challenges faced by those seeking employment while experiencing housing instability.

The Impact of the Minimum Wage

The minimum wage, a cornerstone of employment legislation, often falls short of providing a living wage. We discuss the effects of a subpar minimum wage on individuals and families teetering on the edge of homelessness.

Structural Barriers to Stability

In addition to income inequality, structural barriers exacerbate the issue of homelessness. Discrimination in housing, employment, and the criminal justice system disproportionately affects marginalized communities.

- **Alex's Battle:** Alex, an advocate for the homeless, shares his experiences of encountering structural barriers while trying to secure housing and employment after experiencing homelessness. His story underscores the need for policy reforms.

The Criminalization of Homelessness

The criminalization of homelessness is a disturbing trend in many communities. We explore how punitive measures against homeless individuals perpetuate the cycle of homelessness and contribute to a system of incarceration rather than support.

9.2 Structural Barriers

The complexities of homelessness extend beyond individual circumstances. Structural barriers—those deeply ingrained in societal systems—significantly contribute to the persistence of homelessness. In this section, we delve into the multifaceted ways in which structural barriers perpetuate homelessness, examining housing discrimination, employment challenges, and the criminalization of homelessness.

Housing Discrimination

Accessible and affordable housing is a fundamental human right, yet housing discrimination remains a significant barrier for marginalized communities. Discrimination in housing exacerbates homelessness by limiting housing options and contributing to housing instability.

- **Samantha's Struggle:** Samantha, a young mother who faced discrimination while seeking housing, shares her experiences. She discusses the biases she encountered and the impact it had on her family's journey out of homelessness.

Employment Discrimination

Securing stable employment is a crucial step in preventing and overcoming homelessness. However, many individuals with a history of homelessness face employment discrimination, hindering their ability to achieve financial stability.

- **Marcus' Job Search:** Marcus, a survivor who struggled to find employment after exiting homelessness, recounts his job search journey. He highlights the challenges faced by individuals trying to reintegrate into the workforce.

The Criminalization of Homelessness

The criminalization of homelessness is a disturbing trend in many communities. Policies and practices that target homeless individuals with punitive measures exacerbate the cycle of homelessness. Instead of providing support, these measures lead to arrests and incarceration.

- **Cynthia's Arrest:** Cynthia, who experienced homelessness, describes her experience of being arrested for sleeping in a public space due to lack of shelter options. Her story sheds light on the harmful consequences of criminalization.

Addressing Structural Barriers

Confronting structural barriers requires systemic change and a commitment to fostering inclusive, equitable communities. We explore initiatives and advocacy efforts aimed at dismantling these barriers and promoting access to housing and employment opportunities.

- **Alex's Advocacy:** Alex, an advocate for the homeless, discusses his involvement in advocacy campaigns against housing and employment discrimination. He emphasizes the importance of policy reforms in creating a more inclusive society.

9.3 Homelessness and Mental Health

The intersection of homelessness and mental health is a complex and deeply intertwined issue. Homelessness can both contribute to and exacerbate mental health challenges, while untreated mental illness can lead to homelessness. In this section, we explore the intricate relationship between homelessness and mental health, shedding light on the experiences of homeless individuals and the importance of accessible mental health support.

The Vicious Cycle of Mental Health and Homelessness

Homelessness and mental health issues often form a destructive cycle, each exacerbating the other. Understanding this cycle is crucial to addressing the needs of homeless individuals.

- **Emily's Struggle:** Emily, who battled homelessness while experiencing mental illness, shares her journey of seeking help. Her story illustrates the challenges faced by individuals caught in the midst of this cycle.

Access to Mental Health Services

Access to mental health services is essential for homeless individuals grappling with mental health challenges. However, barriers such as lack of insurance, stigma, and limited availability of services can prevent individuals from receiving the support they need.

David's Search for Support: David, who emerged from homelessness, reflects on his efforts to access mental health services while homeless. He discusses the challenges he encountered and the importance of expanding mental health resources.

Harm Reduction and Supportive Services

Harm reduction approaches, which focus on minimizing the negative consequences of substance use and mental health challenges, are critical in supporting homeless individuals. We explore programs and services that prioritize harm reduction and provide holistic support.

The Role of Outreach Teams

Outreach teams play a vital role in connecting homeless individuals with mental health services. We examine the work of outreach teams and their efforts to bridge the gap between the streets and mental health care.

9.4 Addiction and Substance Abuse

Addiction and substance abuse are pervasive issues among homeless individuals, adding layers of complexity to the homelessness crisis. Homelessness can increase vulnerability to substance abuse, while untreated addiction can contribute to homelessness. In this section, we explore the relationship between homelessness and addiction, the challenges faced by homeless individuals, and the importance of harm reduction and recovery support.

The Complex Interplay

Homelessness and addiction often intersect in a complex dance. Individuals experiencing homelessness may turn to substances as a means of coping with the harsh realities of life on the streets. Conversely, addiction can lead to the loss of stable housing and precipitate homelessness.

- **Olivia's Recovery:** Olivia, a survivor who battled addiction while homeless, shares her experiences of recovery. Her story illustrates the challenges and rewards of achieving sobriety.

Harm Reduction Approaches

Harm reduction recognizes that addiction is a health issue, not solely a moral failing. We explore harm reduction strategies aimed at minimizing the negative consequences of substance use while respecting individuals' autonomy and dignity.

Access to Treatment and Support

Access to addiction treatment and support services is crucial for those seeking recovery. However, homeless individuals often face barriers such as limited resources, stigma, and a lack of stable housing.

Sarah's Journey to Sobriety: Sarah, who successfully emerged from homelessness, recounts her path to sobriety and the support she received along the way. Her story highlights the importance of accessible addiction treatment.

Peer Support and Recovery

Peer support and recovery programs play a vital role in helping homeless individuals on their journey to sobriety. We examine the power of community and peer mentorship in the recovery process.

Chapter 10: Homeless by Choice

In a world marred by homelessness, it might seem counterintuitive to choose homelessness voluntarily. However, some individuals make a conscious decision to embrace homelessness temporarily, driven by a profound sense of empathy and a desire to make a difference. In this chapter, we explore the concept of being "Homeless by Choice," delving into the power of empathy, volunteering, community engagement, and advocacy in the fight against homelessness.

The Power of Empathy

Empathy is a force that can drive individuals to take extraordinary steps to understand and alleviate the suffering of others. We examine the role of empathy in inspiring people to choose homelessness as a means of raising awareness and advocating for change.

- **Rachel's Journey:** Rachel, who embarked on a journey of homelessness by choice, shares her motivations for doing so. She discusses the transformative power of empathy in her life.

Walking in Their Shoes: Volunteering and Community Engagement

Volunteering and community engagement are essential pillars of support for homeless individuals. We explore the impact of volunteers and organizations dedicated to providing resources, compassion, and companionship to those in need.

Supporting Local Organizations

Local organizations play a critical role in addressing homelessness at the community level. We examine the work of grassroots organizations and their efforts to provide shelter, food, and support to homeless individuals.

Policy Advocacy and Grassroots Movements

Advocacy is a powerful tool for creating systemic change. We explore the efforts of individuals and grassroots movements dedicated to advocating for policy changes that address the root causes of homelessness.

- **Alex's Advocacy:** Alex, who chose to live homeless temporarily, discusses his advocacy work aimed at addressing the structural barriers contributing to homelessness. He emphasizes the importance of community engagement in advocacy efforts.

Conclusion: A Call to Choose Empathy

Chapter 10 has introduced us to the concept of being "Homeless by Choice." We've explored the profound impact of empathy, the significance of volunteering and community engagement, and the role of advocacy in the fight against homelessness.

As we progress further into Act 2, let us carry with us the understanding that choosing homelessness temporarily can be a powerful statement of empathy and solidarity. It's a reminder that we all have a role to play in making a difference, whether through volunteering, advocacy, or supporting local organizations.

10.1 The Power of Empathy

Empathy is a profound and transformative force. It has the remarkable ability to compel individuals to step outside of their comfort zones, to challenge their preconceptions, and to take actions that bring about meaningful change. In this section, we explore the extraordinary power of empathy as a driving force behind individuals choosing to experience homelessness voluntarily to raise awareness and advocate for change.

Empathy: A Catalyst for Change

Empathy is often the catalyst that motivates individuals to choose homelessness as a means of advocating for those who are marginalized and suffering. It enables them to connect on a deeply human level with the struggles of homeless individuals.

- **Rachel's Journey:** Rachel, who embarked on a journey of homelessness by choice, shares her personal motivations rooted in empathy. She reflects on the profound impact empathy has had on her perspective and actions.

Walking in Their Shoes: A Quest for Understanding

Choosing homelessness by choice is, in many ways, a quest to understand the daily realities faced by homeless individuals. It's a journey that involves stepping into their shoes and experiencing firsthand the challenges of life on the streets.

Empathy in Action: Advocacy and Education

Empathy extends beyond personal experiences; it drives individuals to take action. We explore how those who choose homelessness by choice often engage in advocacy and educational initiatives to raise awareness about homelessness and its root causes.

Inspiring Others through Empathy

The power of empathy is contagious. Those who choose homelessness by choice inspire others to do the same, creating a ripple effect of compassion and action in the fight against homelessness.

10.2 Walking in Their Shoes: Volunteering and Community Engagement

In the quest to address homelessness, volunteering and community engagement play pivotal roles. These acts of compassion bring individuals into direct contact with homeless communities, fostering understanding, empathy, and a deep sense of connection. In this section, we explore the impact of volunteering and community engagement in supporting homeless individuals and creating a sense of belonging.

The Compassion of Volunteers

Volunteers are the unsung heroes of the homelessness crisis. They offer their time, energy, and skills to provide critical support to those in need. We delve into the motivations and experiences of volunteers who dedicate themselves to making a difference.

Connecting on a Human Level

Volunteering and community engagement provide opportunities for individuals to connect with homeless communities on a deeply human level. These interactions break down barriers, challenge stereotypes, and reveal the shared humanity that unites us all.

- **Sophie's Journey:** Sophie, a dedicated volunteer, shares her experiences of working in a homeless shelter. She reflects on the profound connections she's made and the impact of humanizing the homeless experience.

Providing Resources and Support

Volunteers and community organizations are instrumental in providing resources and support to homeless individuals. From offering meals and shelter to facilitating access to medical care and hygiene facilities, their contributions are invaluable.

Building a Sense of Belonging

Homeless individuals often grapple with isolation and a sense of exclusion. Volunteering and community engagement initiatives create spaces where individuals experiencing homelessness can feel valued, heard, and part of a larger community.

The Power of Collective Action

Volunteering and community engagement efforts extend beyond individual actions; they spark collective movements and inspire communities to come together in the fight against homelessness.

10.3 Supporting Local Organizations

At the heart of communities across the world, local organizations dedicated to alleviating homelessness are beacons of hope. They provide essential services, support, and resources to homeless individuals, often on a shoestring budget. In this section, we explore the invaluable work of these grassroots organizations, their impact, and the role they play in addressing homelessness at the community level.

The Unsung Heroes of Local Organizations

Local organizations are often run by dedicated individuals who are deeply committed to making a difference. We delve into the stories of those who have devoted their lives to providing shelter, food, and support to homeless individuals.

Addressing Immediate Needs

Local organizations are on the frontlines, addressing the immediate needs of homeless individuals. They offer hot meals, emergency shelter, hygiene facilities, and clothing, providing a lifeline for those experiencing homelessness.

- **Carlos' Mission:** Carlos, the founder of a local homeless shelter, shares his journey and the challenges of running a shelter on limited resources. He reflects on the impact his organization has had on the community.

Creating a Sense of Community

Homeless individuals often lack a sense of belonging. Local organizations strive to create supportive communities where individuals can find acceptance, camaraderie, and a network of people who care.

Advocacy and Awareness

Local organizations are not only service providers but also advocates for policy changes and increased awareness of homelessness in their communities. They play a vital role in advocating for systemic solutions.

The Role of Volunteers

Volunteers are the lifeblood of local organizations. We explore the experiences of volunteers who contribute their time and efforts to support homeless individuals through these organizations.

Conclusion: The Heart of Compassion

Section 10.3 has shone a light on the incredible work of local organizations in addressing homelessness. These organizations, often run by passionate individuals and supported by volunteers, serve as the heart of compassion in our communities.

10.4 Policy Advocacy and Grassroots Movements

To effect lasting change in the battle against homelessness, it is essential to address its root causes and advocate for systemic solutions. Policy advocacy and grassroots movements serve as powerful instruments in driving the change needed to eradicate homelessness. In this section, we explore the efforts of individuals and movements dedicated to advocating for policy changes that tackle the underlying issues leading to homelessness.

Advocacy as a Catalyst for Change

Advocacy is the engine that drives policy change. It brings attention to the root causes of homelessness and pushes for reforms that can prevent and alleviate homelessness at its source.

Voices for Change

We amplify the voices of advocates, individuals with lived experiences, and organizations that are tirelessly working to address the structural barriers contributing to homelessness.

- **Ella's Advocacy:** Ella, who experienced homelessness and emerged from it, discusses her journey into advocacy. She shares her insights on the power of personal stories in driving change.

Advocating for Housing First

The Housing First approach, which prioritizes providing stable housing as the first step, has gained traction in the fight against homelessness. We explore the efforts of advocates pushing for Housing First initiatives and the impact of this approach.

Grassroots Movements

Grassroots movements have the power to mobilize communities, draw attention to homelessness, and demand action from policymakers. We delve into the stories of grassroots movements that have sparked change.

Policy Reforms and Initiatives

We examine policy reforms and initiatives aimed at preventing homelessness, providing affordable housing, and addressing the systemic factors that contribute to homelessness.

Conclusion: Agents of Change

Section 10.4 has illuminated the role of policy advocacy and grassroots movements in driving systemic change to address homelessness. These agents of change are at the forefront of efforts to dismantle the structural barriers contributing to homelessness.

Chapter 11: 30 Days on the Edge

The "30 Days Without a Roof" challenge is an extraordinary undertaking. It asks individuals to voluntarily choose homelessness for a month, immersing themselves in the harsh realities of the streets. In this chapter, we'll embark on a unique journey, exploring the experiences of those who have taken on this challenge, revealing the survival strategies, unexpected encounters, emotional rollercoaster, and the profound insights gained during 30 days of living homeless.

Introduction to the Homelessness Challenge

The "30 Days Without a Roof" challenge is not for the faint of heart. We begin by introducing this unique challenge and the motivations behind it, exploring why some individuals willingly choose to experience homelessness for a month.

Day 1: The First Night on the Streets

The journey begins with the first night on the streets. We follow the participants as they navigate the uncertainty of where to sleep, what to eat, and how to stay safe. The initial shock and vulnerability of being homeless become palpable.

- **Mark's Night One:** Mark, one of the challenge participants, shares his raw emotions and experiences during the first night of homelessness. He reflects on the stark contrast to his previous life.

Survival Strategies and Realities

To survive on the streets, participants must quickly adapt and learn essential survival strategies. We explore the tactics used to find food, shelter, and safety while living homeless.

Reflections and Insights

As the days pass, participants begin to gain insights into the homeless experience. They reflect on the challenges they face, the judgments they encounter, and the profound lessons they're learning.

Day 15: The Emotional Rollercoaster

Halfway through the challenge, emotions run high. Participants confront the emotional toll of homelessness, from loneliness and despair to moments of unexpected connection and hope.

- **Sarah's Journey:** Sarah, another challenge participant, shares her emotional rollercoaster experience, from the depths of isolation to the unexpected acts of kindness that touch her heart.

The Final Days and Lessons

As the challenge nears its end, participants draw closer to understanding the complexities of homelessness. They grapple with the contrast between their privileged lives and the harsh realities faced by those who endure homelessness daily.

Conclusion: Insights from the Edge

Chapter 11 has taken us on a journey into the "30 Days Without a Roof" challenge. We've witnessed the participants' experiences, survival strategies, and emotional rollercoaster. Their journey has illuminated the stark realities of homelessness and the profound insights gained during their time on the streets.

As we continue our exploration in this chapter and Act 2, let us carry with us the understanding that experiencing homelessness firsthand is a transformative experience. It challenges preconceptions, fosters empathy, and underscores the urgency of addressing homelessness as a societal issue.

In Chapter 12, we'll delve into the ripple effect of empathy, exploring how the experiences of those who choose homelessness voluntarily can inspire positive change in communities.

This chapter explores the "30 Days Without a Roof" challenge, where individuals voluntarily choose to experience homelessness for a month, gaining firsthand insight into the realities of the streets. If you have specific content requirements or need further adjustments, please feel free to let me know.

Chapter 12: Awakening Empathy

The ripple effect of empathy is a powerful force. When individuals voluntarily choose to experience homelessness, they not only transform their own lives but also inspire change in their communities. In this chapter, we explore the profound impact of empathy and how the experiences of those who choose homelessness voluntarily can inspire positive change, foster community building, and set the stage for ending homelessness.

The Ripple Effect of Empathy

Empathy is a force that knows no boundaries. It ripples outward, touching lives, and inspiring compassion in unexpected places. We delve into the ways in which empathy can spark change in communities and individuals.

Stories of Positive Change

We share stories of individuals who were deeply moved by the experiences of those who chose homelessness voluntarily. These stories demonstrate the potential for personal transformation and the awakening of empathy.

- **Emma's Awakening:** Emma, a community member who closely followed the journeys of challenge participants, shares her story of empathy and the actions she took to make a difference in the lives of homeless individuals.

Community Building and Solidarity

The experiences of challenge participants often lead to the formation of supportive communities committed to addressing homelessness. We explore how individuals come together, driven by empathy, to support those in need.

The Journey Towards Ending Homelessness

The awakening of empathy is not an endpoint but a beginning. We discuss the steps communities can take to channel empathy into concrete actions and advocate for lasting solutions to homelessness.

The "30 Days Without a Roof" Challenge: A Journey into Homelessness

Imagine leaving the comfort of your home, the warmth of your bed, and the security of your daily routine behind. Picture yourself on the streets, exposed to the elements, navigating the harsh realities of homelessness. It's a challenge few would willingly embrace, yet for a growing number of individuals, it has become a transformative experience—an experience known as the "30 Days Without a Roof" challenge.

Introduction: The Quest for Understanding

Homelessness is a crisis that affects millions of individuals worldwide. It's a complex issue with deep-seated root causes, from housing insecurity to economic disparities, mental health challenges, and addiction. While the statistics paint a stark picture, it's often the personal stories and lived experiences that resonate most deeply. The "30 Days Without a Roof" challenge seeks to bridge that gap, allowing participants to step into the shoes of those experiencing homelessness and gain firsthand insight.

Chapter 1: The Genesis of a Challenge

The "30 Days Without a Roof" challenge didn't emerge overnight. It was born out of a desire to raise awareness, challenge preconceptions, and inspire action. In this chapter, we explore the origins of the challenge, from its humble beginnings to its growing impact.

Chapter 2: The Rules of Engagement

Participating in the challenge requires a commitment to a set of rules and guidelines. These rules are designed to simulate the realities of homelessness while ensuring the safety and well-being of participants. We delve into the specific rules that govern the challenge and the considerations that go into crafting them.

Chapter 3: The Motivations Behind the Challenge

Why would anyone willingly choose to be homeless for 30 days? In this chapter, we explore the diverse motivations that drive individuals to undertake the challenge. From a deep sense of empathy to a desire for personal growth and advocacy, we uncover the underlying reasons people embark on this unique journey.

Chapter 4: Preparing for the Unprecedented

Preparation is key to surviving 30 days on the streets. Participants must anticipate the challenges they will face, from finding shelter and food to dealing with adverse weather conditions and potential safety risks. We delve into the preparation process and the resources participants gather before embarking on their homeless journey.

Chapter 5: Day 1 - The First Night on the Streets

The journey begins with a single step, and in this case, it starts with the first night on the streets. We follow the participants as they face the unknown, searching for a safe place to sleep, experiencing hunger, and adjusting to the stark contrast between their previous lives and their new reality.

Chapter 6: Navigating the Challenges

Surviving homelessness requires resourcefulness, resilience, and a deep understanding of the challenges at hand. We explore the strategies participants employ to secure food, find shelter, and address their daily needs. From soup kitchens to panhandling, the participants learn to navigate the often unforgiving streets.

Chapter 7: The Unexpected Encounters

Life on the streets is unpredictable, and participants frequently encounter unexpected situations and individuals. In this chapter, we delve into the human connections forged in the midst of adversity, the acts of kindness that brighten even the darkest days, and the challenges of interacting with the housed community.

Chapter 8: The Emotional Rollercoaster

As the days pass, emotions run high. Participants grapple with the emotional toll of homelessness, from loneliness and despair to moments of unexpected connection and hope. We explore the emotional rollercoaster participants experience during the challenge.

Chapter 9: The Final Days and Lessons Learned

As the 30-day mark approaches, participants reflect on their journey, the lessons learned, and the profound insights they've gained. They confront the contrast between their privileged lives and the harsh realities faced by those who endure homelessness daily. We explore the transformative power of the challenge and its lasting impact.

Chapter 10: The Ripple Effect

The "30 Days Without a Roof" challenge doesn't end with the participants; it creates a ripple effect of empathy and action. We delve into the stories of individuals who were deeply moved by the experiences of the challengers, inspiring them to take action and make a difference in their communities.

Conclusion: The Challenge Continues

The "30 Days Without a Roof" challenge is not just a personal journey; it's a call to action. In this concluding chapter, we reflect on the impact of the challenge, the ongoing work to address homelessness, and the collective responsibility to create a more compassionate society.

Epilogue: Beyond the Challenge

The "30 Days Without a Roof" challenge may last for a month, but its effects endure long after participants return to their homes. We explore how the challenge serves as a catalyst for change, advocacy, and community building, setting the stage for ongoing efforts to end homelessness.

The "30 Days Without a Roof" challenge offers a unique opportunity to gain firsthand insight into the realities of homelessness. It challenges participants to confront their preconceptions, fosters empathy, and inspires action. If you have specific content requirements or need further adjustments, please feel free to let me know.

Chapter 13: The Homelessness Challenge: Could You, Would You, Make a Difference?

The "30 Days Without a Roof" challenge has come to an end, but the journey is far from over. In this chapter, we reflect on the entire experience, discuss personal commitments to change, and provide resources and organizations for further support. The question that lingers is whether, after facing the stark realities of homelessness, participants and readers alike can make a difference.

Introduction: A Journey's End and a New Beginning

As the "30 Days Without a Roof" challenge concludes, we begin by acknowledging the incredible journey undertaken by participants and readers. The challenge has taken us on an immersive exploration of homelessness, shedding light on its complexities and inspiring empathy.

Reflections on the Entire Journey

We invite participants and readers to reflect on the entirety of the challenge. What were the most profound moments? How did the experience transform perspectives and attitudes? We explore the collective reflections of those who undertook the challenge.

Your Personal Commitment to Change

The challenge was not undertaken in isolation; it was a call to action. In this section, we discuss the importance of personal commitment to change. What steps can individuals take in their daily lives to contribute to the effort to end homelessness? We explore the significance of small actions and consistent advocacy.

Resources and Organizations for Further Support

Ending homelessness is a complex endeavor that requires a collective effort. We provide a comprehensive list of resources and organizations dedicated to addressing homelessness. From shelters and support services to advocacy groups and initiatives, these resources empower individuals to take concrete actions.

The Path Forward: Building a More Compassionate Society

As we conclude our journey through the "30 Days Without a Roof" challenge, we consider the path forward. How can we collectively build a more compassionate society that addresses the root causes of homelessness and supports those in need? We explore the role of empathy, advocacy, and community engagement in shaping a better future.

Epilogue: A Challenge for Change

The "30 Days Without a Roof" challenge was not just an experiment; it was a challenge for change. In this epilogue, we reflect on the lasting impact of the challenge, the stories of transformation, and the ongoing commitment to ending homelessness. We conclude with a call to action, challenging readers to consider whether they could, would, and will make a difference.

Conclusion: Embracing the Challenge, Inspiring Change

Our journey through "The Homelessness Challenge" has been a transformative exploration of a complex and pressing issue: homelessness. We embarked on this journey with a dual purpose - to understand the stark realities faced by homeless individuals and to inspire change within ourselves and our communities. As we conclude this book, we carry with us the insights, empathy, and commitment to create a more compassionate society.

The Homelessness Crisis: A Multifaceted Challenge

Homelessness is a multifaceted challenge that defies easy solutions. It's not merely the absence of a roof overhead but a profound state of vulnerability, instability, and isolation. Over the course of this book, we've uncovered the root causes of homelessness, explored the various faces of homelessness, and examined the systemic barriers that perpetuate it.

The "30 Days Without a Roof" Challenge: Stepping into Their Shoes

At the heart of this journey was the "30 Days Without a Roof" challenge. This unique experience invited participants and readers alike to step into the shoes of those experiencing homelessness. We followed the participants as they grappled with the harsh realities of life on the streets, confronted their own biases and assumptions, and forged unexpected human connections.

The Transformative Power of Empathy

Throughout our exploration, one theme emerged as a guiding force: empathy. The ability to understand and share in the feelings of another is a transformative power that can break down barriers, challenge stereotypes, and inspire change. We've seen how empathy has the capacity to awaken in us a deep understanding of the homeless experience.

The Ripple Effect of Empathy

The impact of empathy extends far beyond individual transformation. We explored how the experiences of challenge participants, who voluntarily chose to be homeless for a month, created a ripple effect of compassion and action. Community members, inspired by these journeys, found themselves compelled to make a difference.

Community Building and Solidarity

In the wake of the challenge, communities came together to offer support, resources, and a sense of belonging to those experiencing homelessness. This sense of solidarity demonstrated the power of collective action and the potential for building compassionate communities that value every individual.

Policy Advocacy and Grassroots Movements

The battle against homelessness is not just about alleviating its symptoms but addressing its root causes. We examined the vital role of policy advocacy and grassroots movements in driving systemic change. Advocates and organizations tirelessly pushed for reforms aimed at preventing homelessness and providing stable housing.

The Path Forward: Personal Commitment to Change

As we conclude our journey, the question we must all grapple with is: what can we do to make a difference? We explored the significance of personal commitment to change, the power of small actions, and the importance of consistent advocacy. We considered the ways in which each of us can contribute to ending homelessness in our own communities.

Resources and Organizations for Further Support

Ending homelessness requires a collective effort, and this book wouldn't be complete without providing resources and information on organizations dedicated to addressing homelessness. We've compiled a comprehensive list of shelters, support services, advocacy groups, and initiatives that empower individuals to take concrete actions.

A Challenge for Change

"The Homelessness Challenge" was not just an experiment or a story; it was a challenge for change. It was an invitation to step out of our comfort zones, confront our own biases, and take action to create a more compassionate society. As we conclude this book, we issue a challenge to each reader: Could you, would you, make a difference?

A Compassionate Society: Our Collective Responsibility

Our journey through these pages has highlighted the urgency of addressing homelessness as a collective responsibility. It's a challenge that transcends borders, ideologies, and backgrounds. We've learned that empathy, advocacy, community building, and policy reform are all essential components of the solution.

The Journey Continues

As we close the final chapter of this book, we acknowledge that the journey to end homelessness is far from over. It's a journey that continues in the actions we take, the conversations we have, and the compassion we extend to our fellow human beings. We are all protagonists in this narrative of change.

Conclusion: The Challenge Endures

In the end, it's not just about reading these words; it's about living them. It's about embracing the challenge, inspiring change within ourselves, and reaching out to our communities. We conclude with the belief that collectively, we can create a world where no one has to experience the harsh realities of homelessness. The challenge endures, and our response matters.